Chinese in Steps

步步高中文

Volume I

主编：	George X Zhang	张新生
编者：	Linda M Li	李明芳
	Lik Suen	宣力
	George X Zhang	张新生

CYPRESS BOOKS

Cypress Book Co. UK Ltd.

Chinese in Steps Series
Chinese in Steps Volume One
By George X Zhang, Linda M Li, Lik Suen

Editor: Xian Xu
Cover Design: Wenqing Zhang

First published in Great Britain in September 2005 by **Cypress Book Co. UK Ltd.**
13 Park Royal Metro Centre
Britannia Way
London NW10 7PA
02084530687
02084530709 (Fax)

Find us at www.cypressbooks.com

ISBN 1845700023

Printed in China

Preface

Chinese in Steps is a series course book designed for English-speaking adults who learn Chinese either as part of their degree study at university, or simply as part of their professional or self-development programme for a practical purpose. While aiming to deliver an effective result and an enriching experience of learning Chinese language, it has also taken into consideration the needs of those who seek externally validated qualifications.

Chinese in Steps differs from many other textbooks in its approach to language teaching, and in its conscious effort to make use of adult learners' own rich experiences in learning Chinese. Its approach is based upon on how English-speaking adults learn Chinese and aims to deliver language teaching by resorting to an integrated approach of communicative approach, contrastive analysis and cultural awareness.

Chinese in Steps aims to develop learners' productive communicative competence by focusing on key generic speech patterns and making listening and speaking the core activities of each lesson. The book also aims to develop learners' reading and writing skills with a systematic introduction to relevant knowledge backed up with practice based upon cognitive research, as reading skill is crucial for adult learners to acquire if they expect to use and understand Chinese effectively. The layout of the book is designed to make the contents easy to access and follow. Necessary grammar explanations are given where necessary, but grammatical jargon is kept to a minimum.

Chinese in Steps consists of several stages, each of which has two books. The book structure of the first two stages – Beginners and Lower Intermediate levels – is similar, and these two levels are designed to cover most key speech patterns, fundamental grammatical knowledge and about 900 of the most frequently used characters. By the end of these two stages, learners should have covered enough ground to be able to cope with many everyday life needs in a Chinese-speaking environment.

Chinese in Steps can be used for university Chinese language programmes or non-credit bearing part-time Chinese language courses for adult learners. In terms of the level attainable, the completion of the first two stages will cover enough knowledge and skills to prepare for high GCSE, Intermediate Level in the Asset Language scheme and the initial stages of the Elementary/Intermediate HSK. All the books in the first two stages are accompanied with audio CDs.

Volume I of **Chinese in Steps** is for complete beginners, and has 10 lessons. Each lesson starts with a clear objective, and focuses on four key speech patterns or constructions, which are the core components in developing learners' communicative competence. Grammatical knowledge is spread over the lessons and explained in simple English, often with examples. Apart from the first five lessons in Volume I, which introduce pinyin with plenty of relevant exercises and have 20 Chinese characters in each lesson, the rest of the lessons each introduce 22 characters, which brings the total number of characters to 210 in this volume. The layout of each lesson consists of new vocabulary, speech patterns, dialogues, notes on grammar, a cultural note, exercises, character writing and stroke order, and finally information on Chinese characters.

Chinese is often perceived as a difficult language in Europe, especially Chinese characters, but its difficulty lies primarily in the fact that it is so different from European languages. It is important to have a *relaxed* and *confident* attitude to the learning of the Chinese language. **Chinese in Steps** in many ways endeavours to help learners achieve confidence by gradual introduction to the characteristics of Chinese language as adults learn better and more effectively with a good understanding of what they are doing. Language skill is acquired over a long period of time and with frequent practice. Learning and revising *bit by bit* and practising *constantly* and *frequently* are keys to success for adult learners who usually find it difficult to devote much time to study. So before you start to learn Chinese, it is important to remain relaxed and confident during the learning process, to enjoy the experience of entering a different linguistic world, and to study and practise gradually and frequently what you learn.

The authors would like to thank PC T'ung for his unremitting support and expert advice on the book, and to thank Eun Bahng for her inspirational suggestion for the title of the series. Thanks also go to Robert Chard who has taken painstaking efforts to proofread the book, and to many colleagues and Chinese language learners in SOAS Language Centre and elsewhere for their support in piloting this book and providing useful feedback. Finally, we would also like to express our gratitude to Zhansheng Xia, Xian Xu and Wenqing Zhang of Cypress Book Co. UK Ltd. for their professional dedication and help in the publication of the book series. Of course, any errors are the responsibility of the authors. We would be most grateful if the users of the book could kindly give us their comments and feedback.

目 录 Contents

Introduction to Chinese and Pinyin

The Official Chinese Language

The official Chinese language is called *Hànyǔ*. It is the language of the Han people, the major ethnic group in China. *Hànyǔ* is also widely used in a number of countries and regions in Southeast Asia, and by numerous Chinese communities all over the world. Due to its wide usage, it is also called *Zhōngwén*, *Zhōngguóhuà* and *Huáyǔ*.

Spoken Chinese

China is so big that there are many dialects. The official spoken language is called *Pǔtōnghuà* (common speech) - a spoken language primarily based upon the Beijing and northern phonetic system. It is known as *Guóyǔ* (national language) in Taiwan and Mandarin in the West.

The phonetic systems used to indicate the pronunciations and tones of *Pǔtōnghuà* include *Hànyǔ Pīnyīn*, *Zhùyīnfúhào* and other Romanised phonetic systems. *Hànyǔ Pīnyīn* is the Romanised alphabetical system used in the PR China, while *Zhùyīn* is a system of signs used since 1918 and is still in use in Taiwan. The other Romanised systems such as the Wade-Giles system are mainly used by westerners. The UN and other world organizations are using *Hànyǔ Pīnyīn* as the official phonetic system. This book also uses *Hànyǔ Pīnyīn*.

Chinese Grammar

Chinese is a tonal language that is relatively difficult for westerners, but Chinese grammar is quite simple compared to that of English. Once a character is learned, it will never change its form. There is no conjugation, declension, number agreement, case change etc. However, there are a few things that an English speaker should pay special attention to while studying Chinese. These include word formation, particles, measure words, and above all, word order in Chinese sentences.

Chinese Characters

The Chinese written script is Chinese characters. There are about 7000 characters in modern Chinese. The most frequently used 1,000 characters cover 90% of modern readings; the most frequently used 2,500 characters cover 98.0%; and the most frequently used 3,500 characters cover 99.5%.

There are two kinds of characters in use - simplified characters and complicated characters (also termed traditional characters). Simplified characters are used in the PR China, Singapore, official world organizations and increasingly more in education establishments in the rest of world, while complicated characters are used in Taiwan, Hong Kong, Macao and many Chinese communities overseas. Transition in reading from one to the other does not seem to be a huge problem.

Hànyǔ Pīnyīn

Hànyǔ Pīnyīn is a romanised alphabetical system used to indicate the pronunciation of Chinese characters. A character is usually represented by a syllable. Most of the syllables are composed of an initial and a final, though some may not have initials. There are 21 initials and 36 finals in pinyin .

Initials (consonants)

b	p	m	f	d	t	n
l	g	k	h	j	q	x
z	c	s	zh	ch	sh	r

b, **p**, **m**, **f**, **d**, **t**, **n**, **l**, **g**, **k**, **h**, **s** are pronounced pretty close to those in English. **b**, **d**, **g** are unaspirated, while **p**, **t**, **k** are aspirated. Some attention is needed to the following initials:

j	is like	*jee/jea*	as in jeep and jean
q	is like	*chee*	as in cheese and cheek
x	is like	*shee*	as in sheep and sheet
z	is like	*ds*	as in beds or beads
c	is like	*ts*	as in cheats or meets
zh	is like	*dr*	similar to that in drive or dream
ch	is like	*ch*	as in church and match
sh	is like	*sh*	as in English and wish
r	is similar to "r" but with the tip of the tongue curled up a bit more		

zh-ch-sh are pronounced with the tip of the tongue curled up a bit.

Finals (all are vowels except those ending with "-n" and "-ng")

Single finals

a	as in	*are*
e	as	*er* (British pronunciation)
i	as the letter	*e*
o	as in	*or*
u	as in	*fool*
ü	as in French	*tu*

Compound finals

It is important to note that compound finals must be pronounced as a single syllable, not separately.

	i	u	ü
a	ia	ua	
o		uo	
e	ie		üe
ai		uai	
ei		uei(ui)	
ao	iao		
ou	iou(iu)		
an	ian	uan	üan
en	in	uen(un)	ün
ang	iang	uang	
eng	ing	ueng	
ong	iong		
er			

Tones

Pǔtōnghuà is a tonal language with four tones, they are: 1st tone, 2nd tone, 3rd tone, 4th tone. They are also known respectively as high level tone, high rising tone, low falling rising tone and falling tone. There are some syllables that do not have any tone mark (for example some particle words), and they are called neutral tone.

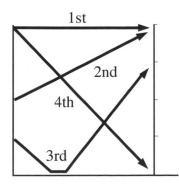

Tone	Mark	Note
1st	*mā*	high level
2nd	*má*	from medium to high
3rd	*mǎ*	from low medium, fall to the bottom and then rise to high
4th	*mà*	from high to the bottom
neutral	*ma*	low flat with no stress

拼音总表 Table – Combination of Initials and Finals in *Pǔtōnghuà* (cont)

	a	o	e	-i	-i	er	ai	ei	ao	ou	an	en	ang	eng	ong	i	ia	iao	ie
	a	o	e			er	ai	ei	ao	ou	an	en	ang	eng		yi	ya	yao	ye
b	ba	bo					bai	bei	bao		ban	ben	bang	beng		bi		biao	bie
p	pa	po					pai	pei	pao	pou	pan	pen	pang	peng		pi		piao	pie
m	ma	mo	me				mai	mei	mao	mou	man	men	mang	meng		mi		miao	mie
f	fa	fo						fei		fou	fan	fen	fang	feng					
d	da		de				dai	dei	dao	dou	dan	den	dang	deng	dong	di		diao	die
t	ta		te				tai		tao	tou	tan		tang	teng	tong	ti		tiao	tie
n	na		ne				nai	nei	nao	nou	nan	nen	nang	neng	nong	ni		niao	nie
l	la		le				lai	lei	lao	lou	lan		lang	leng	long	li	lia	liao	lie
z	za		ze	zi			zai	zei	zao	zou	zan	zen	zang	zeng	zong				
c	ca		ce	ci			cai		cao	cou	can	cen	cang	ceng	cong				
s	sa		se	si			sai		sao	sou	san	sen	sang	seng	song				
zh	zha		zhe		zhi		zhai	zhei	zhao	zhou	zhan	zhen	zhang	zheng	zhong				
ch	cha		che		chi		chai		chao	chou	chan	chen	chang	cheng	chong				
sh	sha		she		shi		shai	shei	shao	shou	shan	shen	shang	sheng					
r			re		ri				rao	rou	ran	ren	rang	reng	rong				
j																ji	jia	jiao	jie
q																qi	qia	qiao	qie
x																xi	xia	xiao	xie
g	ga		ge				gai	gei	gao	gou	gan	gen	gang	geng	gong				
k	ka		ke				kai	kei	kao	kou	kan	ken	kang	keng	kong				
h	ha		he				hai	hei	hao	hou	han	hen	hang	heng	hong				

Some rules about pinyin

1. Chinese characters are monosyllabic, so each character corresponds to an existing syllable. Unlike in English, there are no initial consonant clusters such as "st" or "spr" in Chinese, and liaison is not allowed for two separate syllables as *xī'ān* (two syllables, thus two characters) is completely different from *xiān* (one character).

2. The "*i*" in **zi, ci, si; zhi, chi, shi** and **ri** is not pronounced; the sound is like a vocalic extension of the initial consonant. So the tongue does not move to " i " when pronouncing these sound combinations.

拼音总表 Table – Combination of Initials and Finals in *Pǔtōnghuà*

iu	ian	in	iang	ing	iong	u	ua	uo	uai	ui	uan	un	uang	ueng	ü	üe	üan	ün
you	yan	yin	yang	ying	yong	wu	wa	wo	wai	wei	wan	wen	wang	weng	yu	yue	yuan	yun
	bian	bin		bing		bu												
	pian	pin		ping		pu												
miu	mian	min		ming		mu												
						fu												
diu	dian			ding		du		duo		dui	duan	dun						
	tian			ting		tu		tuo		tui	tuan	tun						
niu	nian	nin	niang	ning		nu		nuo			nuan				nü	nüe		
liu	lian	lin	liang	ling		lu		luo			luan	lun			lü	lüe		
						zu		zuo		zui	zuan	zun						
						cu		cuo		cui	cuan	cun						
						su		suo		sui	suan	sun						
						zhu	zhua	zhuo	zhuai	zhui	zhuan	zhun	zhuang					
						chu	chua	chuo	chuai	chui	chuan	chun	chuang					
						shu	shua	shuo	shuai	shui	shuan	shun	shuang					
						ru	rua	ruo		rui	ruan	run						
jiu	jian	jin	jiang	jing	jiong										ju	jue	juan	jun
qiu	qian	qin	qiang	qing	qiong										qu	que	quan	qun
xiu	xian	xin	xiang	xing	xiong										xu	xue	xuan	xun
						gu	gua	guo	guai	gui	guan	gun	guang					
						ku	kua	kuo	kuai	kui	kuan	kun	kuang					
						hu	hua	huo	huai	hui	huan	hun	huang					

3. The compound final *iou*, *uei*, *uen* are written as *iu*, *ui*, *un* when they form a syllable together with an initial, so *liù*, *guì*, *lún* instead of *liou*, *luei*, *luen*.

4. When there is no initial before finals *i*, *u*, *ü* in a syllable, change *i* into *y* or add *y* in front of *i*; change *u* into *w* or add *w* in front of *u*; add *y* in front of *ü* with the two dots over *ü* omitted. There is a rule guiding the change. If there is only one vowel in the syllable, you can't change but add.

5. The two dots over *ü* are omitted when *ü* appears after **j**, **q** and **x**.

第一课　你好

Learning objectives

Learn and practise pinyin

Learn some useful phrases

Learn basic numbers from 0 to 99

生词　　New Words

你	*nǐ*	pron	you
您	*nín*	pron	you (polite form)
我	*wǒ*	pron	I; me
很	*hěn*	adv	very, rather
好	*hǎo*	adj	good; well
不	*bù*	adv	no, not
谢	*xiè*	v/n	thank; Xie (a surname)
再见	*zàijiàn*	id	bye, see you again　再 again; later　见 see; meet
吗	*ma*	pt	an interrogative particle
0	*líng*	num	zero
一	*yī*	num	one
二	*èr*	num	two
三	*sān*	num	three
四	*sì*	num	four
五	*wǔ*	num	five
六	*liù*	num	six
七	*qī*	num	seven
八	*bā*	num	eight
九	*jiǔ*	num	nine
十	*shí*	num	ten

日常用语　Useful Expressions

A:	你好！	Hello!	B:	你好！	Hello!
A:	您好！	How do you do?	B:	您好！	How do you do?
A:	你好吗？	How are you?	B:	我很好。	I'm very well.
A:	谢谢。	Thank you.	B:	不谢。	Not at all.
A:	再见！	Goodbye!	B:	再见！	Goodbye!

数字　Numbers

0	0	*líng*	11	十一	22	二十二	50	五十
1	一	*yī*	12	十二	23	二十三	60	六十
2	二	*èr*	13	十三	24	二十四	70	七十
3	三	*sān*	14	十四	25	二十五	80	八十
4	四	*sì*	15	十五	26	二十六	90	九十
5	五	*wǔ*	16	十六	27	二十七	...	...
6	六	*liù*	17	十七	28	二十八	95	九十五
7	七	*qī*	18	十八	29	二十九	96	九十六
8	八	*bā*	19	十九	30	三十	97	九十七
9	九	*jiǔ*	20	二十	...	...	98	九十八
10	十	*shí*	21	二十一	40	四十	99	九十九

文化知识 - Cultural Note

中国人的问候　Chinese Greeting

你好 and its more polite form 您好 are common greetings that Chinese use and are appropriate for almost any time of the day. There are similar expressions in Chinese for *good morning*, *good afternoon*, *good evening* and *good night*, but they are not typical. In everyday life Chinese people also use some other expressions as greetings.

练习　Exercises

拼音练习　Pinyin Practice

Listen and repeat after the recording.

1. Tone practice

1)	*mā*	*má*	*mǎ*	*mà*
2)	*tā*	*tá*	*tǎ*	*tà*
3)	*zhī*	*zhí*	*zhǐ*	*zhì*
4)	*jī*	*jí*	*jǐ*	*jì*

2. Sound discrimination

1)	*sī*	*shī*	2)	*cī*	*chī*
3)	*cí*	*chí*	4)	*jí*	*qí*
5)	*zǎo*	*zhǎo*	6)	*nǎo*	*niǎo*
7)	*lüè*	*yuè*	8)	*xiè*	*jiè*

3. Bi-syllables

kāfēi	*Ōuzhōu*	*Bālí*	*Zhōngguó*
zhōngwǔ	*hējiǔ*	*shāngdiàn*	*shēngrì*
míngtiān	*Lúndūn*	*rénmín*	*hóngchá*
píjiǔ	*niúnǎi*	*xuéyuàn*	*róngyì*
zǒngbiān	*tǐcāo*	*huǎnhé*	*běnrén*

jiǎngyǎn	měihǎo	yěwài	zhuǎnbiàn
Yàzhōu	qìchē	lǚchá	sìshí
Shànghǎi	xiàxuě	shàngkè	yùndòng

4. A Chinese Poem – Listen and read aloud.

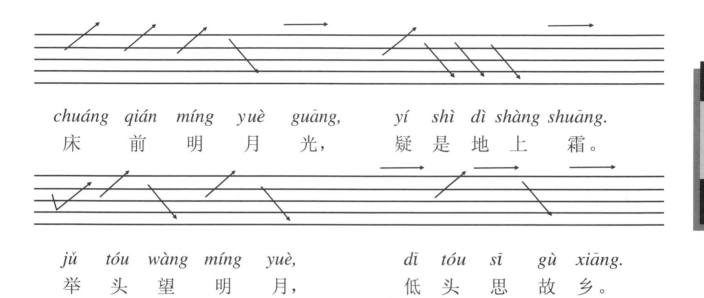

chuáng qián míng yuè guāng,   yí shì dì shàng shuāng.
床　　前　　明　　月　　光，　　　疑　是　地　上　　霜。

jǔ tóu wàng míng yuè,   dī tóu sī gù xiāng.
举　头　望　　明　　月，　　　低　头　思　故　乡。

听力练习　Listening Practice

1. Listen and choose the phrase you have heard in each group.

1)	a. Thank you.	b. How do you do?	c. Hello!
2)	a. Thank you.	b. Goodbye!	c. Not at all.
3)	a. How do you do?	b. I am very well.	c. Not at all.
4)	a. How are you?	b. I am very well.	c. Goodbye!
5)	a. Goodbye!	b. How are you?	c. Not at all.
6)	a. Hello!	b. I am very well.	c. How are you?

2. Number Game

Please listen to the teacher and circle the numbers you have heard.

0	1	2	3	4	5	6	7	8	9
10	11	12	13	14	15	16	17	18	19
20	21	22	23	24	25	26	27	28	29
30	31	32	33	34	35	36	37	38	39
40	41	42	43	44	45	46	47	48	49
50	51	52	53	54	55	56	57	58	59
60	61	62	63	64	65	66	67	68	69
70	71	72	73	74	75	76	77	78	79
80	81	82	83	84	85	86	87	88	89
90	91	92	93	94	95	96	97	98	99

认读练习　　Matching up

Please follow the example and link up each of the Chinese words/phrases with its corresponding pinyin and meaning in English.

再见	*nín hǎo*	sixteen
你好	*zàijiàn*	I am very well
十六	*bāshíqī*	goodbye
你好吗	*wǒ hěnhǎo*	eighty seven
不谢	*nǐ hǎoma*	hello
九十九	*bùxiè*	how are you
您好	*jiǔshíjiǔ*	fifty two
八十七	*shíliù*	how do you do
我很好	*nǐ hǎo*	not at all
五十二	*wǔshí'èr*	ninety nine

汉字知识　**Chinese Characters**

Strokes and Stroke Order　笔划和笔顺

Chinese characters are made up of **strokes**, ranging from one stroke to several dozens. Strokes are typically of eight types, most of which appear in the Chinese character "eternal" (see the Chinese character on the left). The eight strokes are respectively explained and presented as below:

点 (*diǎn*) - a simple dot

横 (*héng*) - a horizontal stroke from left to right

竖 (*shù*) - a vertical stroke from top to bottom

折 (*zhé*) - the bending stroke

提 (*tí*) - a diagonal stroke from lower left to up right

勾 (*gōu*) - a hook usually continued from another stroke

撇 (*piě*) - a diagonal stroke from up right to lower left

捺 (*nà*) - a horizontal stroke, falling from up left to lower right

、
一
丨
ㄱ
㇏
亅
丿
㇏

When writing Chinese characters, there is an order to follow. The correct **stroke order** in writing Chinese characters follows the five basic rules below:

1) From left to right

2) From top to the bottom

3) Left-falling precedes right-falling

4) Horizontal precedes vertical

5) Inside precedes the sealing stroke

女 + 子 = 好

你 + 心 = 您

丿 + 丶 = 人

一 + 丨 = 十

四 + 一 = 四

The stroke order of all the new characters covered in this book is illustrated in the relevant lessons where each of the Chinese characters is presented stroke by stroke in accordance with the above rules.

汉字笔顺 Stroke Order

一	一										
二	一	二									
三	一	二	三								
四	丨	冂	四	四	四						
五	一	丆	开	五							
六	丶	亠	六	六							
七	一	七									
八	丿	八									
九	丿	九									
十	一	十									
你	丿	亻	亻	伫	佁	你					
您	丿	亻	亻	伫	佁	你	你	您	您	您	
不	一	丆	不	不							
很	丿	彳	彳	彳	徂	徂	徂	很	很		
好	乀	夕	女	好	妤	好					
吗	丨	口	口	叩	吗	吗					
再	一	厂	冂	丙	冉	再					
见	丨	冂	贝	见							
我	丿	一	手	手	我	我	我				
谢	丶	讠	讠	讠	讥	谢	谢	谢	谢	谢	谢

写字练习　**Character Writing Exercise**

Can you recognise these characters? Test yourself if you are able to write the pinyin and English meaning on top of each character. Then copy each character following its stroke order on the opposite page. Try to have a feel of the structure of the character when copying, especially those consisting of two or three components.

一					二				
三					四				
五					六				
七					八				
九					十				
不					吗				
再					见				
你					您				
很					好				
我					谢				

第二课　我叫王京

Learning objectives

Introduce your name to others and ask others' name

Introduce a third person by his/her name

Practise and revise pinyin

生词　　New Words

他	tā	pron	he; him
她	tā	pron	she; her
姓	xìng	v	be surnamed
叫	jiào	v	be called; call; shout
贵	guì	adj	honourable; expensive
对	duì	adj	correct; right
也	yě	adv	also; too; neither
什么	shénme	q.w	what　　什 * what　　么 * what
呢	ne	pt	interrogative particle for follow up questions
名字	míngzi	n	name　　名 name　　字 zì character
李	lǐ	n	Li (a surname); plum
李贵	Lǐ Guì	p.n	Li Gui (a name)
王	Wáng	n	Wang (a surname); king
京 *	jīng	n	capital
王京	Wáng Jīng	p.n	Wang Jing (Jim King) (a name)
小	xiǎo	adj	small; young
英 *	yīng	n	hero; Britain
李小英	Lǐ Xiǎoyīng	p.n	Li Xiaoying (a name)
方	fāng	n	Fang (a surname); place
国	guó	n	country
伦 *	lún	n	ethics
方国伦	Fāng Guólún	p.n	Fang Guolun (a name)

句型　　Speech Patterns

S	V	N
我	姓	李。
他	叫	王京。
她	叫	李小英。

S	V	N	吗
你	姓	李	吗？
她	叫	李小英	吗？
他	叫	王京	吗？

S	ADV	ADV	V	N
我		不	姓	李。
他	也	不	姓	李。
她		不	叫	王英。

S	V	QW
他	姓	什么？
她	叫	什么？
你	叫	什么（名字）？

Chinese words do not change forms when used in the sentences no matter where they are. There is no verb conjugation in Chinese.

A statement can be turned into a general question by adding a question particle 吗 and a question mark at the end of the sentence, with a slightly rising tone.

Adverbs always precede the predicate verb. When 也 and 不 appear in the same statement, 也 would occur before 不 to mean " neither".

To ask for specific information, simply put the question word in the place where the information would be in the statement and add a question mark at the end.

补充词汇　　Additional Vocabulary

Chén	陈	a surname	*Bǎoluó*	保罗	Paul
Qián	钱	a surname	*Dàwèi*	大卫	David
Zhāng	张	a surname	*Lìsà*	莉萨	Lisa
Chéng Lóng	成龙	Jackie Chan	*Lùyìsī*	路易丝	Louise
Lǐ Xiǎolóng	李小龙	Bruce Lee	*Mǎlì*	玛丽	Mary
Gǒng Lì	巩俐	Gong Li	*Yuēhàn*	约翰	John

对话 1 Dialogue One

李：您好！

王：您好！

李：您贵姓？

王：我姓王，我叫王京。您贵姓？

李：我姓李，我叫李小英。

对话 2 Dialogue Two

王：你好！

李：你好！

王：你叫什么名字？

李：我叫李贵。

王：我姓王，我叫王京。

李：她叫什么名字？

王：她也姓李，她叫李小英。

李：他呢？

王：他叫方国伦。

语法注释 Grammar Notes

1. **您贵姓？** - A polite idiomatic expression to ask someone's family name. It is usually employed on a formal occasion when you first meet a person, or who is older than you or senior to you. One shouldn't answer it with 贵. For example:

Question: 您贵姓？

Answer: 我姓李。

2. **General questions and answers** - For most of the general questions, you could simply repeat the first verb for "yes" and use 不 plus the first verb for "no". But for questions that contain such verbs as 姓 and 叫, 对 or 不 is used to indicate an affirmative or negative answer, or the full answer should be given. For example:

Question: 你姓王吗？

Affirmative answer: 对。or 我姓王。

Negative answer: 不。or 我不姓王。

3. **呢** - It is another question particle, but used in a follow-up question in a known context without the need to repeat the whole sentence. It is similar to "how about…" or "and you?" in English, for example:

A: 你好吗？

B: 很好，你呢？

A: 我也很好。

文化知识 - Cultural Note

中国人的姓名　Chinese Names

In China, family names always precede the given names. Most commonly seen Chinese family names only have one character though there are some two-character family names. Typically Chinese given names would have two characters. Traditionally one of the characters would indicate the generation to which one belongs to, while the other character would reflect the high hope the parents place on them. Nowadays one-character given names have become very popular.

练习 **Exercises**

拼音练习   **Pinyin Practice**

1. Tone discrimination

1)	*hāo*	*háo*	*hǎo*	*hào*
2)	*jiān*	*jián*	*jiǎn*	*jiàn*
3)	*liū*	*liú*	*liǔ*	*liù*
4)	*zhāng*	*zháng*	*zhǎng*	*zhàng*

2. Read the following family names and names.

1)	*Sūn*	*Zhāng*	*Zhōu*	*Zhū*
2)	*Chén*	*Liú*	*Táng*	*Yáng*
3)	*Kǒng*	*Mǎ*	*Lǔ*	*Lǚ*
4)	*Fàn*	*Mèng*	*Xià*	*Zhào*
5)	*Máo Zédōng*	*Dèng Xiǎopíng*	*Hú Jǐntāo*	*Wēn Jiābǎo*
6)	*Línkěn*	*Ài'yīnsītǎn*	*Bùlái'ěr*	*Bùshí*

3. Listen and circle the pinyin you have heard in each group.

1)	*jiāo*	*xiāo*	2)	*lián*	*nián*
3)	*cī*	*sī*	4)	*zhāng*	*chāng*
5)	*gǎo*	*kǎo*	6)	*lán*	*nán*
7)	*shī*	*sī*	8)	*yuè*	*yè*

听力练习   **Listening Practice**

Listen to the short dialogues and mark if each of the following sentences is true (T) or false (F).

1. His surname is Li.   ( )
2. Her name is Wang Jing.   ( )
3. He is not Fang Guilun.   ( )
4. His surname is Bush.   ( )
5. His name is Wang Gui.   ( )
6. His surname is also Wang.   ( )

▶ 口语练习　　Speaking Practice

1. Introduce yourself in Chinese to another participant, and ask what his/her surname and full name are (the names can be said in English).

2. Walk around the class to introduce yourself and find the full names of at least five of your classmates. Fill in the table below, and then report to the class.

	Family name	Given name
1		
2		
3		
4		
5		

▶ 语法练习　　Grammar Practice

1. Turn the following sentences into negative and general question forms.

　　Example:　　　　我姓李。

　　　　　　　　a.　我不姓李。　　　　b.　你姓李吗？

　1)　我叫李小英。

　2)　你也姓王。

　3)　他叫方国伦。

　4)　他叫王京。

　5)　她姓方。

　6)　她叫李国英。

2. Complete the following dialogues by filling in the blanks with appropriate words given below.

　　Word list:　姓、什么、也、不、对、呢

　1)　A：您贵_____？　　　　　　　B：我姓李。

　2)　A：你叫_____名字？　　　　　B：我叫李小英。

3) A: 她姓王吗？   B: _____，她不姓王。

4) A: 我姓李。您贵姓？   B: 我 _____ 姓李。

5) A: 我叫方国伦，你 _____ ？ B: 我叫李贵。

6) A: 他叫王京吗？   B: _____，他叫王京。

认读练习   Matching up

Please follow the example and link up each of the Chinese words with its corresponding pinyin and meaning in English.

贵姓	*xiǎomíng*	full name
名字	*guìxìng*	UK
不对	*míngzi*	your honourable surname
小名	*Yīngguó*	king
姓名	*búduì*	first name
英国	*guówáng*	not correct
国王	*wángguó*	pet name for a child
王国	*xìngmíng*	kingdom
贵国	*shénme*	what
什么	*guìguó*	your honourable country

翻译练习   Translation

Say the following sentences in Chinese first, and then write them out in characters.

1. What's your honourable surname?
2. My name is Wang Ying, what is yours?
3. What's his name?
4. Her surname is also Li.
5. Are you Fang Guolun? No, I am not Fang Guolun.
6. What is your name? I am called Fang Ying.

汉字知识　**Chinese Characters**

Evolution of Chinese Characters　汉字的演变

Evidence from archaeological discoveries has indicated that Chinese scripts date back as far as over 5000 years ago. These early characters are usually stylised picture of some physical objects presented in horizontal, vertical or curving lines, etched on pottery, carved on turtle shells and bones, on bronze utensils or on bamboo slips. The style of the writing, however, has experienced a lot of changes over thousands of years of evolution, as is illustrated below with the character for horse (*mǎ*), its current form at the bottom of the page is the simplified character (*jiǎntǐzì*) used since the 1950s.

金文: *jīnwén*

Bronze script
15th-11th cent. B.C.

甲骨文: *jiǎgǔwén*

Oracle-bone script
12th-11th cent. B.C.

大篆: *dàzhuàn*

Large-seal script
8th cent. B.C.

小篆: *xiǎozhuàn*

Small-seal script
2nd cent. B.C.

隶书: *lìshū*

Clerical script
2nd cent. A.D.

楷书: *kǎishū*

Regular script
since 4th cent. A.D.

行书: *xíngshū*

Running script
since 4th cent. A.D.

草书: *cǎoshū*

Cursive script
since 4th cent. A.D.

马

简体字: *jiǎntǐzì*

Simplified Chinese
since 1950s

汉字笔顺 Stroke Order

小	亅	小	小				
什	丿	亻	仁	什			
么	丿	幺	么				
王	一	二	王	王			
方	丶	亠	方	方			
叫	丶	口	口	叫	叫		
呢	丶	口	口	叮	叮	呢	呢	呢
也	乛	力	也				
他	丿	亻	仂	仲	他		
她	乚	女	女	如	如	她	
伦	丿	亻	亻	伙	伶	伦	
名	丿	夕	夕	夕	名	名	
李	一	十	才	木	本	李	李
字	丶	宀	宀	宁	宁	字	
英	一	十	艹	艹	苎	苹	英	英
京	丶	亠	六	亠	亠	亨	亨	京
对	乛	又	又	对	对		
姓	乚	女	女	女	如	姓	姓	姓
国	丨	冂	冂	冃	用	国	国	国
贵	丶	一	卩	中	虫	卅	贵	贵	贵

写字练习　Character Writing Exercise

Can you recognise these characters? Test yourself if you are able to write the pinyin and English meaning on top of each character. Then copy each character following its stroke order on the opposite page. Try to have a feel of the structure of the character when copying, especially those consisting of two or three components.

小					方				
什					么				
王					也				
他					伦				
她					姓				
呢					叫				
对					国				
名					字				
李					英				
京					贵				

CHINESE IN STEPS

lesson two

第三课　王先生是英国人

Learning objectives

Introduce where you come from and what your profession is

Ask others for similar details and introduce a third person

Practise and revise pinyin

生词　　New Words

是	shì	v	be	
这	zhè/zhèi	pron	this	
那	nà/nèi	pron	that	
我们	wǒmen	pron	we, us	们 * plural suffix for human nouns
你们	nǐmen	pron	you	
他们	tāmen	pron	they;　them	
先生	xiānsheng	n	Mr; husband	先 first　　生 a person; be born
太太	tàitai	n	Mrs; wife	太 wife; too (excessive)
小姐	xiǎojie	n	Miss	姐 jiě elder sister
老师	lǎoshī	n	teacher	老 old　　师 master
医生	yīshēng	n	doctor	医 medicine; to cure
人	rén	n	person, people	
中国	Zhōngguó	p.n	China	中 middle
英国	Yīngguó	p.n	UK	
地方	dìfang	n	place	地 place; earth
北京	Běijīng	p.n	Beijing	北 north
伦敦	Lúndūn	p.n	London	敦 * honest
都	dōu	adv	all, both	
就	jiù	adv	exactly	
谁	shuí/shéi	q.w	who	
哪	nǎ/něi	q.w	which	

句型　　　Speech Patterns

S	是	N
这	是	李小姐。
那	是	王先生。
她	是	方太太。

The Chinese verb 是 links two "equivalent" parts here, and is pronounced in a neutral tone.

S	是	N
我们	是	医生。
你们	是	老师。
他们	是	中国人。

Nouns do not change form no matter whether they are singular or plural.

S	是	QW (+N)
你	是	哪国人？
她	是	什么地方人？
他	是	谁？

As you learned in Lesson 2, Chinese question words could be at any place in the sentence, depending on which part of the information you ask about.

S	是不是	N
你	是不是	李英？
他	是不是	老师？
他们	是不是	中国人？

An affirmative-negative choice question is formed with the "verb + not + verb" construction plus a question mark at the end of the sentence.

补充词汇　　Additional Vocabulary

Fǎguó	法国	France	*gōngchéngshī*	工程师	engineer
Bālí	巴黎	Paris	*gōngwùyuán*	公务员	civil servant
Déguó	德国	Germany	*jìzhě*	记者	journalist
Bólín	柏林	Berlin	*jīnglǐ*	经理	manager
Rìbìn	日本	Japan	*lùshī*	律师	lawyer
Dōngjīng	东京	Tokyo	*kuàiji*	会计	accountant

◇ **对话 1**   **Dialogue One**

王：您好，我叫王京。

李：您好，我叫李小英。

王：李小姐是哪国人？

李：我是中国人。

王：您是中国什么地方人？

李：我是北京人。王先生是不是英国人？

王：是，我是伦敦人。

◇ **对话 2**   **Dialogue Two**

方：王老师，这是李小姐。李小姐，这是王老师。

李：您好，王老师。

王：你好，李小姐。

方：王老师，李小姐也是北京人。

王：是吗？我们都是北京人。

方：那是谁？那是不是您太太？

王：是，那就是我太太。

李：王太太也是老师吗？

王：不，她是医生。

语法注释　Grammar Notes

1. 们 - It makes pronouns plural when added to them, such as 我们, 你们, 他们 and 她们. However, while this suffix can also be added to nouns referring to a group of professionals such as 老师们, it can't be used for animals, or a group of people where there is a numeral modifier before such nouns.

2. **Answering an affirmative-negative choice question** - simply use the verb for "yes" or 不 plus verb for "no". For example:

　　Question: 你是不是中国人？

　　Affirmative answer: 是。

　　Negative answer: 不是。

3. 都 - 都 can be used to refer to "both" and "all". It is an adverb, and never goes before a noun or pronoun. When it is used with 不, the position of 都 before or after 不 would affect the meaning of the sentence. For example:

　　我们都不是老师。 None of us is a teacher. (total negation)

　　我们不都是老师。 Not all of us are teachers. (partial negation)

4. 那就是我太太 - 就 is here for the sake of emphasis, meaning "surely" or "exactly". For example, when someone who doesn't know you is looking for you and calling out your name, you could step forward and say, 我就是.

文化知识 - Cultural Note

中国人的称谓　How Chinese address each other

As a mark of respect, Chinese usually address each other by their profession or official position, which is attached as a suffix to the family name. So you hear 李老师 (Teacher Li), 王医生 (Doctor Wang) and so on. Other common titles include 先生, 太太, 小姐 and they are used as a formal but general mode of address when one is unsure of the other's position or profession. Those who know each other well would add the prefix 老 or 小 before the family name to form informal terms of address e.g.老李, 小王. The choice of prefix is generally age related. Given names are usually used among family members, close friends, classmates and colleagues.

练习 Exercises

拼音练习　Pinyin Practice

1. Sound discrimination

1)	*yā*	*yē*	*yāng*	*yōu*
2)	*qié*	*qiáo*	*qiú*	*qué*
3)	*shǎn*	*shǎng*	*shěn*	*shěng*
4)	*rè*	*ruò*	*rào*	*ròu*

2. Read the following city and country names.

1)	*Tiānjīn*	*Kūnmíng*	*Xiānggǎng (HK)*	*Lāsà*
2)	*Wúxī*	*Héféi*	*Táiběi*	*Chóngqìng*
3)	*Guǎngzhōu*	*Jǐnán*	*Hǎikǒu*	*Wǔhàn*
4)	*Guìzhōu*	*Dàlián*	*Shànghǎi*	*Dàqìng*
5)	*Xībānyá (Spain)*	*Hélán (Holland)*	*Mǎdélǐ (Madrid)*	*Ài'ěrlán*
6)	*Nuówēi (Norway)*	*Éluósī (Russia)*	*Bǐlìshí (Belgium)*	*Mòsīkē (Moscow)*

3. Listen and circle the pinyin you have heard in each group.

1)	*chāng*	*shāng*	2)	*jiǔ*	*zǒu*
3)	*chù*	*qù*	4)	*xiàn*	*shàn*
5)	*jué*	*qué*	6)	*lǜ*	*lù*
7)	*róng*	*lóng*	8)	*luǎn*	*nuǎn*

听力练习　Listening Practice

Listen to the short dialogues and mark if each of the following sentences is true (T) or false (F).

1.	Her surname is Li.	( )
2.	Teacher Xie is French.	( )
3.	Mr Wang is from London.	( )
4.	Mrs Wang is a doctor.	( )
5.	Miss Fang is not from Britain.	( )
6.	Not all of them are Chinese.	( )

▶ 口语练习　**Speaking Practice**

1. Work in pairs or small groups to introduce to each other who you are and where you are from.

2. Please introduce to others someone you know with the following professions.

Family name	Given name	Profession	Country	City
		yīshēng (doctor)		
		lǎoshī (teacher)		
		lǜshī (lawyer)		
		gōngchéngshī (engineer)		
		jīnglǐ (manager)		

▶ 语法练习　**Grammar Practice**

1. Turn the following sentences into choice questions (CQ) or special questions (SQ).

Example: 我姓王。　　你姓什么？＿＿＿＿＿＿＿ (SQ)

　　　　　　　　　　你姓不姓王？＿＿＿＿＿＿ (CQ)

1) 他叫李贵。　＿＿＿＿＿＿＿＿＿＿＿ (SQ)

2) 我是英国人。　＿＿＿＿＿＿＿＿＿ (CQ)

3) 王小姐是伦敦人。　＿＿＿＿＿＿＿ (SQ)

4) 你老师是中国人。　＿＿＿＿＿＿＿ (CQ)

5) 那是方小姐。　＿＿＿＿＿＿＿＿＿ (SQ)

6) 我们是医生。　＿＿＿＿＿＿＿＿＿ (CQ)

2. Complete the following dialogues by filling in the blanks with appropriate words given below.

Words list: 哪、什么、都、不、谁、不是

1) A: 你是 _____ 国人？   B: 我是英国人。

2) A: 他是 _____ ？   B: 他是方老师。

3) A: 你们是 _____ 是伦敦人？   B: 我们是伦敦人。

4) A: 她是 _____ 地方人？   B: 她是北京人。

5) A: 你们都是中国人吗？   B: 我们不 _____ 是中国人。

6) A: 他是不是医生？   B: _____ ，他是老师。

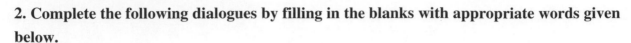

认读练习   **Matching up**

Please follow the example and link up each of the Chinese words with its corresponding pinyin and meaning in English.

中医	*míngrén*	old people
生字	*rénmíng*	northerner
生人	*shēngrén*	new character
老人	*běifāngrén*	name of a person
名人	*zhōngyī*	north
人名	*lǎorén*	Chinese medicine
北方	*shēngzì*	famous people
北方人	*běifāng*	stranger
姐姐	*zhōngyī yīshēng*	Chinese medical doctor
中医医生	*jiějie*	elder sister

翻译练习　Translation

Say the following sentences in Chinese first, and then write them out in characters.

1. Which country are you from?
2. Who is he? He is the very person - Teacher Wang.
3. This is Miss Fang. She is also from Beijing.
4. That is Mr Li. He is a doctor.
5. We are all British.
6. None of them are teachers.

汉字知识　Chinese Characters

Pictographic Characters　象形字

A pictograph is a graphic depiction of a physical object. Most early Chinese characters discovered through archaeological findings were like "pictures" of objects. Characters in the middle column of the table below are a result of long years of evolution of the respective pictographs in the left column. Could you guess the English meaning for the corresponding Chinese character in the column on the right?

Pictographs and their evolution	Character	English
	日 *rì*	
	月 *yuè*	
	山 *shān*	
	水 *shuǐ*	
	鸟 *niǎo*	

汉字笔顺 Stroke Order

人	丿	人								
们	丿	亻	亻	们	们					
中	丶	冂	口	中						
北	丨	十	丬	才	北					
太	一	一	大	太						
先	丿	一	生	生	先	先				
生	丿	一	一	牛	生					
老	一	十	土	少	耂	老				
师	丨	丿	广	圹	师	师				
这	丶	二	亍	文	文	讠	这			
那	丁	刁	刁	男	那	那				
是	丶	口	曰	日	旦	早	早	昱	是	
地	一	十	土	圫	地	地				
医	一	丆	医	三	至	天	医			
姐	乀	女	女	如	如	姐	姐	姐		
哪	丶	口	口	叼	叼	叼	明	哪	哪	
都	一	十	土	少	耂	者	者	者	都	都
谁	丶	讠	讠	讣	讣	讣	诈	诈	谁	谁
就	丶	二	亍	亠	京	京	京	京	尌	就	就
敦	丶	二	六	亩	亩	亯	亨	享	亨	敦	敦

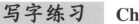 写字练习　**Character Writing Exercise**

Can you recognise these characters? Test yourself if you are able to write the pinyin and English meaning on top of each character. Then copy each character following its stroke order on the opposite page. Try to have a feel of the structure of the character when copying, especially those consisting of two or three components.

人					中					
太					是					
先					生					
老					师					
北					地					
们					这					
医					姐					
那					哪					
都					谁					
就					敦					

第四课　今天几号？

Learning objectives

Tell and ask the date, month and day of the week

Talk and ask about age and birthday

Practise and revise pinyin

生词　New Words

今天	jīntiān	t.w	today	今 * today, this 天 day, sky
明天	míngtiān	t.w	tomorrow	明 next; bright
今年	jīnnián	t.w	this year	年 year
九月	jiǔyuè	t.w	September	月 month; moon
十一月	shíyīyuè	t.w	November	
星期	xīngqī	n/m.w	week	星 star　期 period
星期二	xīngqī'èr	t.w	Tuesday	
生日	shēngrì	n	birthday	日 day (formal); sun; Japanese
号	hào	n	day; number; size	
弟弟	dìdi	n	younger brother	弟 younger brother
妹妹	mèimei	n	younger sister	妹 younger sister
岁	suì	m.w/n	year (age); time	
快乐	kuàilè	adj	happy	快 pleased; fast　乐 happy
大	dà	adj	big; old	
几	jǐ	q.w	how many (used for less than 10)	
多	duō	q.w/adj	how many/much; many, much	
的	de	pt	an attributive and possessive particle	
吧	ba	pt	an interrogative or suggestive particle	
对不起	duìbuqǐ	id	sorry, pardon	起 * rise

句型　　　Speech Patterns

S	ADV	是	Day/Date
今天		（ 是 ）	二号。
今天	不	是	星期天。
明天	不	是	九月十号。

The verb 是 is often omitted when talking about time and date in Chinese, especially in spoken Chinese. But 是 is not omitted when 不 is there.

S	是	QW
今天	（ 是 ）	几号？
今天	（ 是 ）	星期几？
明天	（ 是 ）	几月几号？

Please note that the special question word 几 is used to ask about the day and date, not 什么.

S	TW	ADV	是	NUM	岁
我弟弟				九	岁。
我姐姐	今年			二十	岁。
我	今年	不	是	十八	岁。

When talking about age, the verb 是 is usually omitted. Again, it cannot be omitted when an adverb 不 is present.

S	TW	QW
你弟弟	今年	几岁？
你姐姐		多大？
你	今年	多大？

When asking about age, 几岁 is usually used for children, while 多大 is for adults.

补充词汇　　　Additional Vocabulary

Days of the week: 星期 + number (except Sunday)						
星期一	星期二	星期三	星期四	星期五	星期六	星期日 / 天
Name of the months: number + 月						
一月	二月	三月	四月	五月		六月
七月	八月	九月	十月	十一月		十二月

对话 1　　**Dialogue One**

李：王京，今天星期几？

王：今天星期二。

李：今天几号？

王：二十三号。

李：九月二十三号，明天是我弟弟的生日。

王：是吗？他今年几岁？

李：他今天八岁，明天九岁。

王：我妹妹今年也九岁。

李：她的生日是哪天？

王：十一月七号。

对话 2　　**Dialogue Two**

王：李英，你的生日是几月几号？

李：11 月 14 号。

王：11 月 14 号，明天就是 11 月 14 号吧？

李：对。明天就是我的生日。

王：生日快乐！

李：谢谢。你的生日是哪天？

王：我的生日是 9 月 18 号。

李：你今年多大？

王：我今年 20 岁。

语法注释　Grammar Notes

1. **Attributive/Possessive marker** 的 - It is used to indicate a possessive relationship between the two parts, like "'s" in English. When the relationship is closely personal, and the "owner" is in the form of a pronoun, this marker is often omitted.　For example:

李英是我姐姐。Li Ying is my elder sister.

方先生是王京的老师。Mr Fang is Jim King's teacher

2. **生日是哪天？** - 哪天 is similar in meaning to 几月几号, and it is more colloquial.

3. **吧** - A question particle that usually indicates the expectation of the speaker for a positive reply. If not certain at all, 吗 is used instead. For example:

明天是五号吧？　Tomorrow is the 5th, isn't it?

明天是五号吗？　Is tomorrow the 5th?

4. **日／号 and 日／天** - 号 and 日 are both used to refer to date. 号 is a more colloquial while 日 is formal. Similarly, 星期天 is more colloquial than 星期日 and thus is used more often in everyday life.

5. **The Date and its reading and writing in Chinese** - The date in Chinese starts with the largest unit (year) and ends on the smallest unit (day). While the month and date can be written in Arabic numbers, the number showing the day of the week is never written in that way.

English	Chinese	
05/09	9月5日	九月五日
10/1914	1914年10月	一九一四年十月
1966	1966年	一九六六年
28/04/1935	1935年4月28日	一九三五年四月二十八日
Fri. 06/08/2004	2004年8月6日星期五	二〇〇四年八月六日星期五

文化知识 - Cultural Note

中国人看数字   Chinese Numbers

As in all other cultures, numbers from 1 to 9 also have cultural connotations in Chinese. For instance, Chinese regard 6 and 8 as lucky numbers, as 6 signifies "smooth" and 8 rhymes with the word "get rich" (*fā*). 4 is regarded as an unlucky number because it sounds similar to the word "death" (*sǐ*). 9 is a magic and powerful number, as it is the highest amongst the single digit numbers. So it has the meaning of "many" as is found in English.

练习   Exercises

拼音练习   Pinyin Practice

1. Sound discrimination

1)	*sūn*	*suān*	*sān*	*sāng*
2)	*chóng*	*chóu*	*chún*	*cháo*
3)	*lǎo*	*liǎo*	*lǒu*	*luǒ*
4)	*zuì*	*zài*	*zàn*	*zuàn*

2. Read the following professions and titles.

1)	*gōngrén*	(worker)	*nóngmín*	(peasant)
2)	*yǎnyuán*	(actor/tress)	*hùshi*	(nurse)
3)	*kēxuéjiā*	(scientist)	*shùxuéjiā*	(mathematician)
4)	*shòuhòuyuán*	(saleman/woman)	*fúwùyuán*	(waiter/tress)
5)	*xiàozhǎng*	(head of a school)	*chǎngzhǎng*	(head of a factory)
6)	*dǒngshìzhǎng*	(chairman of the board)	*zǒngtǒng*	(president of a state)

3. Listen and circle the pinyin you have heard in each group.

1)	*jīn*	*qīn*	2)	*xīn*	*yīn*
3)	*róu*	*lóu*	4)	*yóu*	*móu*
5)	*liǎo*	*niǎo*	6)	*miǎo*	*xiǎo*
7)	*cùn*	*xùn*	8)	*jùn*	*hùn*

听力练习　Listening Practice

Listen to the short dialogues and choose the correct answer for each question.

1. a) 十月一号　　b) 十月十一号　　c) 十一月一号
2. a) 二月二十一日　　b) 十二月七日　　c) 二月十七日
3. a) 星期一　　b) 星期二　　c) 星期三
4. a) 英国人　　b) 伦敦人　　c) 中国人
5. a) 六月二十九号　　b) 六月九号　　c) 九月六号
6. a) 我姐姐的　　b) 我妹妹的　　c) 我弟弟的

口语练习　Speaking Practice

1. Work in pairs and ask each other questions about the days and dates for today and tomorrow.

2. Suppose the following dates are the birthdays of someone you know. Could you please tell others a bit more about them (their name, age, profession, nationality etc.) ?

1) 14 Jan 1955
2) 29 March 1983
3) 31 July 1978
4) 28 Nov 2004

语法练习　Grammar Practice

1. Ask questions about the underlined parts in the following sentences.

Example:　她的生日是明天。　　她的生日是哪天？

1) 我的生日是九月十五号。
2) 我妹妹今年十岁。
3) 今天星期六，明天星期天。
4) 明天是李老师的生日。

5) <u>星期三</u>是小李的生日。

6) 王老师是<u>中国北京人</u>。

2. Complete the following dialogues by filling in the blanks with appropriate words given below.

  Word list:　多、的、几、三月六号、明天、几岁

1) A: 你的生日是几月几号？　　B: 我的生日是 ＿＿＿＿ 。

2) A: 你弟弟今年 ＿＿＿＿ ？　　B: 八岁。

3) A: 明天是你 ＿＿＿＿ 生日吗？　B: 不是。

4) A: 她 ＿＿＿＿ 大？　　　　　　B: 她今年十九岁。

5) A: 今天六号。　　　　　　　　B: ＿＿＿＿ 七号。

6) A: 今天星期 ＿＿＿＿ ？　　　B: 今天星期四。

　　认读练习　　**Matching up**

Please follow the example and link up each of the Chinese words with its corresponding pinyin and meaning in English.

年年	*míngxīng*	elderly people
明月	*suìyuè*	time
明星	*zhōngniánrén*	everyone
老年人	*míngyuè*	medium size
中年人	*niánnián*	star (celebrities)
大号	*lǎoniánrén*	middle-aged people
小号	*dàhào*	bright moon
岁月	*rénrén*	every year
人人	*zhōnghào*	big size
中号	*xiǎohào*	small size

翻译练习 **Translation**

Say the following sentences in Chinese first, and then write them out in characters.

1. What's the date today?
2. Today is your birthday. Happy birthday!
3. How old are you?
4. It is 2005 this year. The next year is 2006.
5. What day is tomorrow? It is Saturday tomorrow.
6. Who is he? He is my younger sister's teacher.

汉字知识 **Chinese Characters**

Indicative Characters 指事字

Indicative characters make use of some indicative sign to refer to an implied idea. Compared to a pictographic character, they are more abstract and symbolic.

There are two types of indicatives. One is composed of a pictograph and an indicating sign. For examples, the character for knife and its derivative for knife-edge.

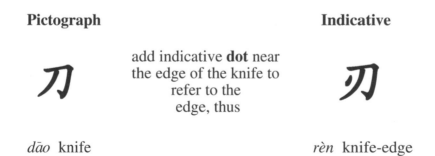

Pictograph		Indicative
刀	add indicative **dot** near the edge of the knife to refer to the edge, thus	刃
dāo knife		*rèn* knife-edge

The other type of indicatives is constructed purely of abstract strokes to indicate a meaning. For example, 一, 二 and 三 are used to indicate one, two, and three. A slightly more abstract pair of indicatives are positional words, as shown below.

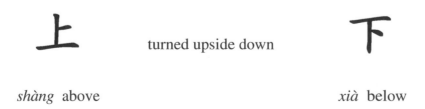

上	turned upside down	下
shàng above		*xià* below

汉字笔顺 Stroke Order

几	丿	几									
大	一	ナ	大								
天	一	二	天	天							
日	丨	冂	日	日							
月	丿	冂	月	月							
今	丿	人	亽	今							
号	丶	口	므	呈	号						
明	丨	冂	月	日	明	明	明	明			
的	丿	亻	白	白	白	的	的	的			
年	丿	仁	仁	仨	年	年					
多	丿	夕	夕	多	多	多					
快	丶	忄	忄	忙	忙	快	快				
乐	一	匚	乐	乐	乐						
吧	丨	口	口	叩	叩	吧	吧				
岁	丨	屮	山	岁	岁	岁					
弟	丶	丷	屮	兰	弟	弟	弟				
妹	乚	女	女	女	妒	妹	妹	妹			
起	一	十	土	卡	走	走	起	起	起		
星	丶	冂	曰	曰	尸	早	星	星	星		
期	一	十	廿	甘	甘	其	其	其	期	期	期

写字练习　Character Writing Exercise

Can you recognise these characters? Test yourself if you are able to write the pinyin and English meaning on top of each character. Then copy each character following its stroke order on the opposite page. Try to have a feel of the structure of the character when copying, especially those consisting of two or three components.

几				今				
大				天				
日				月				
明				的				
号				年				
岁				多				
快				乐				
弟				妹				
吧				起				
星				期				

第五课 他天天晚上都写汉字

Learning objectives

To say one does something

To say one does something at a particular time

Practise and revise pinyin

生词　　New Words

学	*xué*	v	learn, study	
做	*zuò*	v	make, do	
写	*xiě*	v	write	
看	*kàn*	v	see, watch, look; read	
喝	*hē*	v	drink	
上网	*shàngwǎng*	v-o	surf the net	上 go on; on　网 net
专业	*zhuānyè*	n	major, subject	专 specialised　业 course; industry
英文	*yīngwén*	n	English language	文 (written) language
中文	*zhōngwén*	n	Chinese language	
文学	*wénxué*	n	literature	
电视	*diànshì*	n	TV	电 electricity, electric　视 vision; watch
书	*shū*	n	book	
汉字	*hànzì*	n	Chinese character	汉 Chinese
晚上	*wǎnshang*	t.w	evening	晚 late
早上	*zǎoshang*	t.w	morning	早 early
茶	*chá*	n	tea	
牛奶	*niúnǎi*	n	(cow) milk	牛 cow; bull　奶 milk
还是	*háishì*	conj	or (for question)	还 still
天天	*tiāntiān*	t.w	every day	

句型　　Speech Patterns

S	V	O
我	学	中文。
你	看	书。
我们	上	网。

For sentences with action verbs, Chinese is the same as English in S-V-O order.

S	TW	ADV	V	O
我	晚上		写	汉字。
你们	天天	都	上	网。
她	明天	不	看	电视。

It is important to remember that the time word always goes before verbs.

S	TW	ADV	V	O
你	今天晚上		做	什么？
你	天天早上	都	做	什么？
她	明天晚上		看	电视吗？

It is simple to turn the above statements into questions, either by using a question word, or simply adding a question particle.

S	V	O₁	还是	V	O₂
你	看	中文书	还是	看	英文书？
你	学	中文	还是	学	法文？
他	是	老师	还是		医生？

还是 links two choices to form an alternative question, but it is not used with question words or question particles. Please note that 还是 is not used in a statement either.

补充词汇　　Additional Vocabulary

Fǎwén	法文	French	*zuòfàn*	做饭	cook (a meal)
Déwén	德文	German	*kāfēi*	咖啡	coffee
Rìwén	日文	Japanese	*jiǔ*	酒	alcoholic dink
kàn diànyǐng	看电影	watch movies	*kělè*	可乐	cola
kàn xiǎoshuō	看小说	read novels	*guǒzhī*	果汁	fruit juice
zuò zuòyè	做作业	do homework	*kuàngquánshuǐ*	矿泉水	mineral water

对话 1　　**Dialogue One**

方：你好，我叫方京。

李：你好，我叫李英。

方：你学什么专业？

李：我学中文。你呢？

方：我学英国文学。你今天晚上做什么？

李：我写汉字。

方：你明天晚上做什么？

李：我写汉字。

方：你天天晚上都写汉字吗？

李：对。你晚上都做什么？

方：我看书、看电视、上网。

对话 2　　**Dialogue Two**

李：小王，你喝不喝茶？

王：我早上不喝，谢谢。

李：你早上喝什么？

王：我喝牛奶。你喝牛奶吗？

李：我不喝牛奶，早上晚上我都喝茶。

王：你喝中国茶还是英国茶？

李：我喝中国茶。

语法注释   Grammar Notes

1. **你天天晚上都写汉字吗？** - 都 is used here to emphasise "every evening" when the action 写汉字 takes place. 都 can be used in a special question with 什么 such as 你都喝什么 in an expectation to have a list of things in the reply (semantically plural). However, 都 is not needed when replying unless the objects are placed before the verb. For example:

   A: 你都喝什么？

   B: 我喝牛奶，也喝英国茶。or 牛奶、英国茶我都喝。

2. **她明天不看电视** - The negation 不 in this sentence should be put after the time word. But if the time word refers to frequency such as 天天, 不 should go before the time word.

   Compare: 她今天不写汉字。

   　　　　　她不天天写汉字。

3. **还是** - Please note that this choice word in the sense of "or" is only used in questions, not in statements.

4. **Tone changes** are usually for the sake of economy when speaking. We have already come across quite a few. For example, 不 has a fourth tone, but it becomes a second tone when followed by another fourth tone, as in 不看 and 不谢. A third tone should become a second tone when it is immediately followed by another third tone, for instance, 你好. Tone changes are only pronounced, but usually not marked in pinyin.

文化知识 - Cultural Note

中文的语序   Word Order in Chinese

Unlike in English, time words in Chinese must be placed before the verb. In fact this is true of place nouns too as you will soon learn. This difference reflects how the two languages perceive an action. English is action oriented, so the key elements for a S-V-O sentence run one after another closely while time and place words follow at the end. Chinese, however, seems to focus on the process in which an action actually takes place. In another word, an action usually takes place in a specific time at a specific place, thus all these elements in a sentence precede the action of the verb. For example, 我天天晚上写汉字.

练习　Exercises

拼音练习　Pinyin Practice

1. Sound discrimination

1)	*jiǔ*	*jiǎo*	*jiǎ*	*jiě*
2)	*shēn*	*shān*	*shuān*	*shuāng*
3)	*zuǒ*	*zǒu*	*suǒ*	*sǒu*
4)	*chuò*	*cuò*	*suò*	*shuò*

2. Read the following names of public places.

1)	*chāoshì*	(supermarket)	*yóujú*	(post office)
2)	*jiǔbā*	(pub)	*fànguǎnr*	(restaurant)
3)	*fēijīchǎng*	(airport)	*túshūguǎn*	(library)
4)	*tíngchēchǎng*	(car park)	*bówùguǎn*	(museum)
5)	*huǒchēzhàn*	(train station)	*měiróngtīng*	(beauty saloon)
6)	*yuèlǎnshì*	(reading room)	*diànyǐngyuàn*	(cinema)

3. Listen and circle the pinyin you have heard in each group.

1)	*dìtú*	*dìtóu*	2)	*diàotóu*	*dàlóu*
3)	*sānshí*	*sàngshī*	4)	*shǒushì*	*shuòshi*
5)	*chángzhēng*	*Chángchéng*	6)	*chánghóng*	*chánglóng*
7)	*jiǎnfà*	*jiěfàng*	8)	*jiǎnhuà*	*jiǎnghuà*

听力练习　Listening Practice

Listen to the short dialogues and mark if each of the following sentences is true (T) or false (F).

1.	She studies Chinese.	( )
2.	She will watch TV tonight.	( )
3.	Li Ying's major is English literature.	( )
4.	Wang Jing studies Chinese on Sunday evenings.	( )
5.	She drinks milk in the morning.	( )
6.	She writes characters in the morning.	( )

口语练习   Speaking Practice

1. Work in pairs to find out what each other does every day in a week by following the example. You may use English for the part of the answer.

Q: 你星期一早上做什么？   A: 我星期一早上 go to work。

Q: 你星期一晚上做什么？   A: 我星期一晚上看电视。

星期	早上	晚上
星期一		
星期二		
星期三		
星期四		
星期五		
星期六		
星期日		

2. Work in pairs and find out what each other drinks during the day.

语法练习   Grammar Practice

1. Please insert the given word in the right place in each sentence.

Example: 她不喝英国茶。（早上）

她早上不喝英国茶。

1) 英国人喝英国茶吗？   （都）

2) 你看电视吗？   （今天晚上）

3) 她上网。   （天天）

4) 我们学英国文学。   （不）

5) 他不喝中国茶，我不喝中国茶。   （也）

6) 这是谁茶？   （的）

2. Complete the following dialogues by filling in the blanks with appropriate words given below.

Word list:　　还是、写、中文、喝、都、上网

1) A: 你学什么专业？　　　　　　B: 我学 _____ 。

2) A: 你晚上 _____ 做什么？　　　B: 上网、看电视。

3) A: 你明天晚上做什么？　　　　B: 我 _____ 汉字。

4) A: 你看中文书 _____ 看英文书？　B: 我看英文书。

5) A: 你早上喝牛奶吗？　　　　　B: _____ 。

6) A: 你晚上 _____ 吗？　　　　　B: 不上。

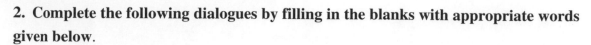

认读练习　　**Matching up**

Please follow the example and link up each of the Chinese words with its corresponding pinyin and meaning in English.

奶牛	*zhōngxué*	milk cow
奶茶	*rìwén*	middle school
电网	*nǎichá*	students
日文	*dàxué*	university
小学	*nǎiniú*	tea with milk
中学	*diànwǎng*	primary school
大学	*xuéshēng*	Japanese language
学生	*xiǎoxué*	electricity grid
一星期	*shàngxué*	go to school
上学	*yī xīngqī*	one whole week

翻译练习　　**Translation**

Say the following sentences in Chinese first, and then write them out in characters.

1.　What is your major? I study English literature.
2.　What do you do on Saturdays?
3.　Do you drink tea or milk?
4.　Ms Wang writes Chinese characters every evening.
5.　I don't drink Chinese tea in the morning.
6.　Do you read or watch TV in the evening?

汉字知识　　**Chinese Characters**

Ideative Characters (1)　　会意字（一）

Ideatives are also called associative compounds because as the name suggests, they are usually made up of two or more independent characters. The meaning of an ideative is normally derived from the meanings of its constituent characters.

There are two types of ideative characters. The first type of ideatives consists of two or more of the same characters to express the idea of multiplicity or quantiy, as illustrated below:

Character 1	+	**Character 2**	=	**Ideative**
人 *rén* people		人 *rén* people		从 *cóng* follow
人 *rén* people		从 *cóng* follow		众 *zhòng* masses

If 木 is a pictograph for a **tree**, guess what the other two Chinese characters below mean respectively?

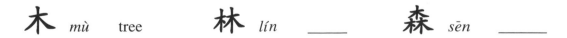

木 *mù* tree　　　　林 *lín* _____　　　　森 *sēn* _____

汉字笔顺 Stroke Order

上	丨	上	上								
文	丶	二	亠	文							
书	㇕	乛	书	书							
汉	丶	冫	氵	汈	汉						
专	一	二	专	专							
业	丨	业	业	业	业						
写	丶	冖	写	写	写						
牛	丿	二	二	牛							
奶	㇛	女	女	奶	奶						
早	丶	冂	日	日	旦	早					
还	一	丁	不	不	不	还	还				
学	丶	丷	丷	丷	兴	学	学	学			
看	一	二	三	手	手	看	看	看	看		
电	丶	冂	日	日	电						
视	丶	冫	礻	礻	礼	视	视	视			
网	丨	冂	冈	冈	网	网					
茶	一	艹	艹	艹	艾	苓	苓	茶	茶		
晚	丨	冂	日	日	旷	昒	昒	晗	晬	晚	
喝	丨	口	口	吲	吲	吲	吲	喝	喝	喝	喝
做	丿	亻	亻	什	什	估	估	做	做	做	做

写字练习　Character Writing Exercise

Can you recognise these characters? Test yourself if you are able to write the pinyin and English meaning on top of each character. Then copy each character following its stroke order on the opposite page. Try to have a feel of the structure of the character when copying, especially those consisting of two or three components.

上						文					
书						早					
牛						电					
汉						还					
专						业					
茶						学					
看						写					
网						奶					
视						晚					
喝						做					

第六课　我会说一点儿汉语

Learning objectives

Talk about what one likes or dislikes to do

Talk about what one can do or should do

Talk about one's favourite sports

生词　　　　New Words

会	*huì*	m.v/n	can, may; meeting		
想	*xiǎng*	m.v/v	would like to, intend; think; miss		
应该	*yīnggāi*	m.v	should	应 should	该 should
喜欢	*xǐhuan*	m.v/v	like	喜* like	欢 * *huān* happy
认识	*rènshi*	v	know	认 recognise	识 *shí* know
说	*shuō*	v	speak		
打	*dǎ*	v	play (games); beat		
踢	*tī*	v	kick; play (football)		
汉语	*hànyǔ*	n	Chinese language	语 language	
外语	*wàiyǔ*	n	foreign language	外 outside; foreign	
日语	*rìyǔ*	n	Japanese language		
法语	*fǎyǔ*	n	French	法 France; law; method	
足球	*zúqiú*	n	football	足 foot	球 ball
网球	*wǎngqiú*	n	tennis		
篮球	*lánqiú*	n	basketball	篮 basket	
一点儿	*yīdiǎnr*	n	a bit	点 point; hour	儿 non-syllabic suffix
可是	*kěshì*	conj	but	可 may, can	
为什么	*wèishénme*	q.w	why	为 for, on account of	
一起	*yīqǐ*	adv	together		
因为	*yīnwèi*	conj	because	因 cause, reason for	

句型　　Speech Patterns

S	MV	V	O
我	会	说	汉语。
你	应该	学	中文。
她	喜欢	打	篮球。

S	MV	不 MV	V	O
你	会	不会	说	汉语？
他	想	不想	打	网球？
他	喜欢	不喜欢	踢	足球？

S	MV	不 MV	V	O
他	应该	不应该	学	外语？
他	应	不应该	学	汉语？
他	喜	不喜欢	踢	足球？

S	TW	ADV	V	好吗
我们	今天		看电视，	好吗？
我们		一起	写汉字，	好吗？
我们		一起	上网，	好吗？

Modal verbs are used here in pretty much the same way as in English. That is, the modal verb goes before the action verb.

When there is a modal verb in an affirmative-negative choice question, it is the modal verb that takes the affirmative-negative form rather than the action verb.

When the modal verb is a two-character word, you can repeat just the first character in an affirmative-negative choice question to make the sentence shorter.

好吗 is used at the end of a statement to make a suggestion.

补充词汇　　Additional Vocabulary

Sports (with action verb 打)

dǎ páiqiú	打排球	play play volleyball
dǎ pīngpāngqiú	打乒乓球去	play table tennis
dǎ yǔmáoqiú	打羽毛球	play badminton
dǎ gǎnlǎnqiú	打橄榄球	play rugby
dǎ shuǐqiú	打水球	play water polo

Sports (with other action verbs)

huábīng	滑冰	skate
huáshuǐ	滑水	go surfing
huáxuě	滑雪	ski
pǎobù	跑步	go jogging
yóuyǒng	游泳	swim

对话 1　　**Dialogue One**

李：王京，你是英国人，为什么想学汉语？

王：我喜欢学外语。我会说法语，也会说一点儿日语。

李：你会说日语！？你认识汉字吗？

王：不认识。

李：我会说一点儿汉语，可是我也不认识汉字。

王：你想学汉字吗？

李：我的老师说我应该学，可是我不想学。

王：为什么？

李：我喜欢汉字，可是汉字不喜欢我。

对话 2　　**Dialogue Two**

王：小李，你喜不喜欢打篮球？

李：不喜欢，我喜欢踢足球。

王：你喜欢打网球吗？

李：我喜欢看，不喜欢打。

王：为什么？

李：因为我不太会打。

王：我也不太会，我们一起学，好吗？

李：好。

语法注释 　**Grammar Notes**

1. **认识** - The word is used in the sense of having the knowledge and skill to "recognise" or "identify " though it is often translated as "know" in English. There is another Chinese word for "know" in the sense of "having a knowledge of something". 认识 is normally used for knowing people, characters and roads. For example:

我不认识汉字。　I don't know Chinese characters.
我不认识他。　I don't know him personally.

2. **一点儿** - Some Chinese words have additional 儿 added to them esp. when spoken, but this 儿 doesn't form an independent syllable. It is usually pronounced as "r" as part of the syllable in front of it. In some cases, it distinguishes the meaning of the words. For instance:

这 (zhè) means "this"　　　这儿 (zhèr) means "here"
那 (nà) means "that"　　　那儿 (nàr) means "there"

3. **我不太会打（网球）** - I don't play (tennis) very well. 太 means too much, and is similar to 很 here, though slightly more in terms of degree.

CHINESE IN STEPS
lesson six

文化知识 - **Cultural Note**

"天" 字的魅力　**Charm of the Character 天**

天 is an indicative character that reflects the way the Chinese in ancient times viewed the relationship between human being and the sky (Heaven) above. The character signifies the unity of people (as 大 means "big" showing a person with the arms fully stretched horizontally) and the heaven above (as indicated by the character 一 on top referring to the sky). Many of the words in today's Chinese language consisting of the character 天 are usually associated with a sense of predetermined destiny, authority, innate nature or quality etc.

练习　Exercises

口语练习　Speaking Practice

Work in pairs or small groups, using modal verbs to talk about.

1. What you can do or cannot do (speak a foreign language, cooking etc);

2. What you like to do and dislike to do;

3. Please ask and answer the following questions in Chinese:

A	B
What is your name?	Are you from Beijing?
Where are you from?	Do you drink milk in the morning?
When is your birthday?	Is tomorrow your birthday?
What do you drink in the morning?	Are you going to play tennis tonight?
What is your major (study)?	Is your major Chinese literature?
What are you going to do tomorrow?	Do you know our English teacher or not?
Shall we play tennis together tonight?	Do you play tennis or football?
Would you like to watch TV tonight?	Do you watch TV every evening?
Do you like to read or surf on line?	Do you read or write tonight?
I can speak Chinese, what about you?	Can't you speak English?

听力练习　Listening Practice

1. Listen and repeat, pay attention to the tones of 不 in the last line.

1)	*a. bù shuō*	*b. bù hē*	*c. bù tī*
2)	*a. bù xué*	*b. bù lái*	*c. bù yóuyǒng*
3)	*a. bù hǎo*	*b. bù dǎ*	*c. bù xǐhuan*
4)	*a. bù shì*	*b. bù kàn*	*c. bù rènshi*

2. Listen to the short statements or dialogues and mark if each of the following sentences is true (T) or false (F).

1) Xiao Li should know how to write Chinese characters. 　( )

2) She likes to play basketball, but she does not like to play tennis. ( )

3) Teacher Wang doesn't know Japanese at all. ( )

4) He can recognize Chinese characters, but can't write them. ( )

5) He drinks Chinese tea every morning. ( )

6) He is going to watch TV this evening. ( )

语法练习 Grammar Practice

1. Match the following verbs with the given words (verbs may be used more than once).

Verb list：学、看、打、喝、写、说、踢、上

1) _____ 汉语   2) _____ 足球   3) _____ 网球

4) _____ 电视   5) _____ 汉字   6) _____ 网

7) _____ 中国茶   8) _____ 篮球   9) _____ 法语

10) _____ 牛奶   11) _____ 书   12) _____ 老师

2. Complete the following sentences by filling in the blanks with appropriate words given below.

Word list：喜欢、可是、一点儿、踢、打、会

1) 我会说 _____ 英语。

2) 我们今天 _____ 网球，好吗？

3) 她会说汉语，_____ 她不认识汉字。

4) 你想学 _____ 足球吗？

5) 我 _____ 上网，可是我太太不喜欢上网。

6) 我们都 _____ 说英语。

Matching up

Please follow the example and link up each of the Chinese words with its corresponding pinyin and meaning in English.

英语	yīngyǔ	there
地球	Fǎguó	English
法国	nǎr	viewpoint
法人	fǎrén	study of law
法学	nàr	the Earth
看法	shīshēng	teachers & students
师生	zhèr	France
那儿	dìqiú	where
哪儿	fǎxué	legal person
这儿	kànfa	here

翻译练习 ## Translation

Say the following sentences in Chinese first, and then write them out in characters.

1. My Chinese teacher doesn't like to play football.
2. She can't speak French, but she can speak Japanese.
3. I 'd like to learn Chinese characters.
4. Doctor Li can speak a little Chinese.
5. He surfs the net every evening.
6. I would like to have some Chinese tea.

阅读 ## Reading

你晚上都做什么？

你们好！我的中文名字叫李大明，我是法国人，今年十九岁，是伦敦大学的学生。我的专业是汉语和中国文学。我会说法语、英语、汉语和一点儿日语。我很喜欢学外语，我也很喜欢打球。我星期一晚上打篮球，星期二晚上看法文书，星期三晚上打网球，星期四晚上学中文，星期五晚上踢足球，星期六晚上上网看中国电影(diànyǐng-film)，星期天晚上我写汉字。你们晚上都做什么？

Please answer the following questions based on the information in the text above.

1. Who is Li Daming and where is he from?
2. How old is he and what is his major?
3. What languages can he speak?
4. What does he do on Thursday and Friday evenings?
5. What do you do in the evenings?

汉字知识　Chinese Characters

Ideative Characters (2)　会意字（二）

The second type of ideative usually consists of two different characters to express an idea that "combines" the meanings of the constituent characters. For example:

Character 1		+	Character 2		=	Ideative		
人	rén / person		木	mù / tree		休	xiū	rest
小	xiǎo / small		土	tǔ / soil		尘	chén	dust
手	shǒu / hand		目	mù / eye		看	kàn	look

Some ideative characters are culturally defined, as illustrated below:

Character 1		+	Character 2		=	Ideative		
田	tián / field		力	lì / strength		男	nán	man
女	nǚ / woman		子	zǐ / children		好	hǎo	good
人	rén / people		言	yán / speech		信	xìn	trust

汉字笔顺 Stroke Order

儿	丿	儿									
点	丶	卜	广	占	占	占	点	点			
足	丶	口	口	甲	甲	昆	足				
因	丨	冂	円	円	因	因					
为	丶	力	为	为							
可	一	一	一	可	可						
外	丿	夕	夕	列	外						
打	一	十	扌	扌	打						
会	丿	人	스	스	会	会					
认	丶	讠	讠	认							
识	丶	讠	讠	沢	识	识	识				
应	丶	二	广	广	应	应	应				
该	丶	讠	讠	讠	讱	诙	该	该			
说	丶	讠	讠	讠	讱	词	说	说	说		
法	丶	丶	氵	汇	汁	法	法	法			
语	丶	讠	讠	讱	语	语	语	语	语		
喜	一	十	士	吉	吉	吉	吉	吉	壴	喜	喜	喜
欢	丁	又	汉	欢	欢	欢						
想	一	十	才	木	相	相	相	相	相	想	想	想
篮	丿	广	广	竺	竹	竺	筲	筲	篮	篮	篮	
球	一	二	干	王	玎	玎	玎	玎	球	球	球	
踢	丨	口	甲	甲	足	足	趴	趴	踢	踢	踢	

写字练习　Character Writing Exercise

Can you recognise these characters? Test yourself if you are able to write the pinyin and English meaning on top of each character. Then copy each character following its stroke order on the opposite page. Try to have a feel of the structure of the character when copying, especially those consisting of two or three components.

儿						足					
因						为					
可						会					
点						应					
法						外					
打						球					
认						识					
说						语					
该						想					
喜						欢					
篮						踢					

第七课　你们有北京烤鸭吗？

Learning objectives

Order simple food and drinks in a restaurant

Talk about your likes and dislikes for certain foods

Learn to use some of the Chinese measure words

生词　　New Words

有	yǒu	v	have; there be		
要	yào	v/m.v	want		
吃	chī	v	eat		
点	diǎn	v	order		
白酒	báijiǔ	n	liquor	白 white	酒 alcoholic drink
红酒	hóngjiǔ	n	red wine	红 red	
啤酒	píjiǔ	n	beer	啤 * beer	五星啤酒 Five Stars Beer
烤鸭	kǎoyā	n	roast duck	烤 roast; bake	鸭 duck
牛肉	niúròu	n	beef	肉 meat	
红烧肉	hóngshāoròu	n	braised meat in soy sauce	烧 cook; braise	
炒饭	chǎofàn	n	stir-fried rice	炒 stir fry	饭 rice, food
白菜	báicài	n	Chinese cabbage	菜 vegetable; dish; food	
青菜	qīngcài	n	green vegetable	青 green	
法国	Fǎguó	p.n	France		
有名	yǒumíng	adj	famous		
好吃	hǎochī	adj	delicious		
没	méi	adv	negation word for 有		
只	zhǐ/zhī	adv/m.w	only; m.w for birds and some other animals		
个	gè	m.w	a general measure word		
瓶	píng	m.w/n	bottle of; bottle		
杯	bēi	m.w/n	glass of, cup of; cup		
碗	wǎn	m.w/n	bowl of; bowl		
盘	pán	m.w/n	dish of, plate of; plate		

句型 Speech Patterns

S	有	O
他们	有	烤鸭。
我们	有	中文书。
她	有	电视。

有 means "to have" in English, but it is also used to means "there exists" as you will see in the next lesson.

S	没 （有）	O
他	没 （有）	姐姐。
你	没 （有）	中国茶。
我们	没 （有）	啤酒。

It is important to note that the negative form of 有 is 没有. It is common to omit 有 in 没有 in spoken Chinese.

S	V	NUM	MW	O
我	要	（一）	杯	啤酒。
我们	要	三	碗	炒饭。
他	要	（一）	只	烤鸭。

In Chinese most nouns cannot be modified by the number directly, and a measure word is needed between the noun and the number. While the number can be omitted if it is "one", the measure word can't.

S	V	NUM	MW	O
我	点	（一）	个	青菜。
我们	点	（一）	只	烤鸭。
我	点	（一）	瓶	红酒。

点 is a verb here. It means "to order". It originally refers to ordering something by pointing one's finger to it.

补充词汇 Additional Vocabulary

hóng pútaojiǔ	红葡萄酒	red wine	*sānmíngzhì*	三明治	sandwich
bái pútaojiǔ	白葡萄酒	white wine	*dàngāo*	蛋糕	cake
júzhi zhī	橘子汁	orange juice	*dànchǎofàn*	蛋炒饭	egg-fried rice
píngguǒ zhī	苹果汁	apple juice	*chǎomiàn*	炒面	stir-fried noodle
hóngchá	红茶	black tea	*jiǎozi*	饺子	jiaozi
lǜchá	绿茶	green tea	*shuǐguǒ*	水果	fruit

对话 1　　**Dialogue One**

W：你们好！你们想喝点儿什么？

李：有没有中国白酒？

W：对不起，我们只有中国红酒。

谢：我们今天就喝中国红酒吧。

W：你们要几瓶？

王：我们只有四个人，先要一瓶吧。

W：好，你们想吃点儿什么？

方：你们有北京烤鸭吗？

W：有。我们这儿的北京烤鸭很有名。

李：你们这儿还有什么好吃的？

W：我们的红烧肉也很好吃。

谢：好，我们要一个红烧肉、一只烤鸭。

王：再点一个炒青菜、一个牛肉炒白菜、四碗炒饭。

对话 2　　**Dialogue Two**

W：先生，您想吃点儿什么？

李：我要一盘牛肉炒饭。

W：好。您想喝点儿什么？

李：有啤酒吗？

W：有。英国啤酒、中国啤酒，我们都有。

李：有没有中国五星啤酒？

W：有。

李：我要一杯五星啤酒。

语法注释   Grammar Notes

1. **Measure word** - Chinese nouns all require a certain measure word before them when used in a context involving numbers. Measure words exist in English, but usually with uncountable nouns such as the underlined words in a <u>cup</u> of tea; a <u>bottle</u> of water; and a <u>flock</u> of sheep etc. Like in English, some Chinese measures are shared by groups of nouns while others are used only with some nouns. So you have to pay special attention to measure words when learning Chinese nouns.

2. 你们想喝点儿什么？ - What would you like to drink? Please note the difference between 想 and 要. The latter is much more direct while the former would soften the tone of speaking, making it sound more polite.

3. 先来一瓶吧 - 先 is an adverb here meaning first. It can be used together with 再 to indicate the sequencer of two actions. For example, 我们先喝酒，再吃饭。

4. 好吃 and 好喝 - The meaning of each word is very obvious, referring to "good to eat" and "good to drink". This construction (adj + verb) is common in Chinese, and the new compound is usually an adjective, or stative verb as is called in some other books.

5. **More tone change** - 一 is pronounced with a first tone on its own, but it becomes a fourth tone when it precedes a first tone, a second tone or a third tone syllable (e.g. *yī zhī; yī pán; yī běn*). Like 不, 一 becomes a second tone when it precedes a fourth tone syllable (e.g. *yī gè*). However, as mentioned before, such tone changes are pronounced, but not marked in pinyin

文化知识 - Cultural Note

中国人的饮食   Food in Chinese Life

Food remains an important aspect of Chinese life. If you just look around in China, you would see many Chinese restaurants. For years, food was a concern for the state as well as common folks. As a result, eating is still a major event in many traditional Chinese celebrations, such as the New Year, weddings, birthday parties, and indeed friends' get-togethers. In fact, it is so pervasive that asking someone if she or he has eaten is still a casual greeting one often hears amongst the Chinese people.

练习 Exercises

口语练习 Speaking Practice

1. Work in pairs and talk about what kind of drink and food you like.

2. Here is a menu. Work in a small group. Pretend you are at a Chinese restaurant with one of you as a waiter or waitress. Now try to order something from him or her.

菜单 （ *càidān* –MENU ）

中国红酒	杯／瓶	法国红酒	杯／瓶
英国啤酒	杯／瓶	五星啤酒	杯／瓶
中国白酒	杯／瓶	可乐	杯／瓶
烤鸭	只	炒牛肉	个／盘
炒青菜	个／盘	红烧肉	个／盘
牛肉炒饭	个／盘	炒饭	个／碗

听力练习 Listening Practice

1. Listen and repeat, pay attention to the tone of 一.

1)	一杯中国茶	2)	一只烤鸭
3)	一盘青菜	4)	一瓶啤酒
5)	我会说一点儿中文	6)	我们一起学汉字
7)	一个中国人	8)	一个英国人

2. Listen to the short dialogues and choose the right answer for each question.

1)	a. roast duck	b. white wine	c. fried rice
2)	a. British beer	b. Chinese red wine	c. Chinese beer
3)	a. stir-fried beef	b. braised meat in sauce	c. roast duck
4)	a. beer	b. English tea	c. Chinese tea
5)	a. Japanese books	b. Chinese books	c. English books
6)	a. his birthday	b. her birthday	c. They like roast duck

语法练习　**Grammar Practice**

1. Choose the correct word in A, B or C to complete each of the following sentences.

1)　我们要三 ＿＿＿＿＿＿ 炒饭。

　　a. 杯　　　　　b. 瓶　　　　　c. 盘

2)　老王和他太太都 ＿＿＿＿＿＿ 会说英语。

　　a. 不　　　　　b. 喜欢　　　　c. 没

3)　我要一 ＿＿＿＿＿＿ 啤酒。

　　a. 杯　　　　　b. 只　　　　　c. 盘

4)　我 ＿＿＿＿＿＿ 一只烤鸭。

　　a. 想　　　　　b. 喜欢　　　　c. 要

5)　王小明 ＿＿＿＿＿＿ 有弟弟。

　　a. 不　　　　　b. 没　　　　　c. 都

6)　英国酒好喝，可是英国菜不太 ＿＿＿＿＿＿ 。

　　a. 好喝　　　　b. 好吃　　　　c. 喜欢

2. Use 没 and 不 to change the following sentences into negative form.

1)　今天我们有烤鸭。

2)　我要日本啤酒。

3)　你喜欢踢足球吗？

4)　他们有中国茶。

5)　他天天看电视。

6)　我们今天晚上写汉字。

认读练习　**Matching up**

Please follow the example and link up each of the Chinese words with its corresponding pinyin and meaning in English.

早饭	*zǎofàn*	wine glass
晚饭	*hǎokàn*	good looking
茶杯	*chábēi*	breakfast
酒杯	*yāròu*	supper
酒瓶	*fànwǎn*	duck meat
酒会	*jiǔpíng*	tea cup
饭碗	*jiǔbā*	wine bottle
酒吧	*wǎnfàn*	pub
鸭肉	*jiǔbēi*	rice bowel/job
好看	*jiǔhuì*	wine party

翻译练习　**Translation**

Say the following sentences in Chinese first, and then write them out in characters.

1. Do you have Chinese beer? I would like to have a glass.
2. We don't have stir-fried beef with green vegetable today.
3. Tomorrow is my birthday, shall we eat Chinese?
4. I like to drink Chinese beer and eat Beijing roast duck.
5. We would like to have four bottles of French red wine.
6. I like French food very much, as it is very delicious.

阅读　**Reading**

我喜欢吃中国饭

你们好！你们认识我，我是李大明。我很喜欢吃中国饭、喝中国茶。
我天天喝中国茶，可是我很少 (*hěnshǎo* - seldom) 吃中国饭，因为我不会做。

我很想学，可是没有老师。我的中文老师也不会做，她说她<u>家</u> (jiā - home)
她先生做饭，她只会吃，不会做。上个星期六我们老师家有一个<u>晚会</u>
(party)。晚会上有很多好吃的饭菜。中国菜有北京烤鸭、红烧牛肉、炒
饭，还 (in addtion) 有炒青菜。英国菜有烤牛肉和<u>三明治</u> (sānmíngzhì -
sandwich)。有的人 (some people) 吃英国饭、有的人吃中国饭，有的人英国
饭、中国饭都吃，可是我只吃中国饭，因为我喜欢吃中国饭。

Please answer the following questions based on the information in the above text.

1. What does Li Daming like to eat and drink?
2. Why does he seldom have Chinese food?
3. Is Daming's Chinese teacher a good cook?
4. What kinds of food were there at the party?
5. Who only ate Chinese food at the party and why?

汉字知识 Chinese Characters

Phonetic-semantic Compounds 形声字

A phonetic-semantic compound is also referred to as pictophonetic. It usually consists of a
semantic radical (which could be a pictograph) and a phonetic element. Characters constructed in
this way represent well over half of the frequently used Chinese characters (different statistics
claim from 60% to about 90%).

Semantic radicals can be independent characters or symbols. Semantic radicals indicate a
semantic field, or what they are associated with. The phonetic element – sometimes an
independent character on its own, provides some clue to the pronunciation of the compound.

Sementic radical/meaning	Phonetic component	P-S compounds	Meaning - pinyin
氵 - water	曷 hé	渴	thirsty - kě
口 - mouth	曷 hé	喝	drink - hē
火 - fire	少 shǎo	炒	stir fry - chǎo

汉字笔顺　Stroke Order

个	ノ	人	个							
只	丶	口	口	尸	只					
白	ノ	亻	白	白	白					
红	乙	纟	纟	纟	红	红				
吃	丨	口	口	叫	吃	吃				
肉	丨	冂	内	内	肉	肉				
有	一	ナ	冇	有	有	有				
没	丶	冫	氵	氿	沪	没	没			
炒	丶	丷	火	火	灼	灼	炒	炒		
饭	ノ	𠂊	饣	饣	饭	饭	饭			
杯	一	十	才	木	杧	杯	材	杯		
要	一	冖	亓	西	西	覀	要	要	要	
青	一	二	圭	主	丰	青	青	青		
菜	一	艹	艹	艹	苹	苹	苹	苹	苹	苹	菜
烧	丶	丷	火	火	炉	炂	烂	烧	烧	
烤	丶	丷	火	火	火	灶	灶	烤	烤	烤
鸭	丨	冂	日	日	甲	甲	甲	甲	鸭	鸭
啤	丨	口	口	呭	呬	呬	呬	咱	啤	哩	啤
酒	丶	冫	氵	沪	汇	沔	洒	洒	酒	
瓶	丶	丷	兰	兰	羊	并	并	瓶	瓶	瓶
盘	ノ	丿	冂	内	舟	舟	舟	舟	舟	盘
碗	一	丆	石	石	矿	矿	矿	矿	矿	碗

写字练习　Character Writing Exercise

Can you recognise these characters? Test yourself if you are able to write the pinyin and English meaning on top of each character. Then copy each character following its stroke order on the opposite page. Try to have a feel of the structure of the character when copying, especially those consisting of two or three components.

个						白					
只						有					
肉						要					
青						菜					
杯						吃					
啤						红					
酒						没					
炒						饭					
烧						烤					
鸭						盘					
瓶						碗					

第八课　我家有四口人

Learning objectives

Talk about your family

Say if you are tired or thirsty

Offer something to eat or drink

生词　　New Words

累	*lèi*	adj	tired	
忙	*máng*	adj	busy	
渴	*kě*	adj	thirsty	
饿	*è*	adj	hungry	
爸爸	*bàba*	n	dad	爸 dad
妈妈	*māma*	n	mum	妈 mum
家	*jiā*	n	home; family; house; specialist in a field	
男朋友	*nán péngyou*	n	boyfriend	男 man, male　朋 / 友 *yǒu* / 朋友 friend
女朋友	*nǚ péngyou*	n	girlfriend	女 woman, female
哥哥	*gēge*	n	elder brother	哥 elder brother
作家	*zuòjiā*	n	writer	作 do; make; write
工作	*gōngzuò*	n	work	工 work; labour
商人	*shāngrén*	n	businessman	商 business; commercial
学生	*xuésheng*	n	student	
律师	*lǜshī*	n	lawyer	律 law; rule
狗	*gǒu*	n	dog	
猫	*māo*	n	cat	
条	*tiáo*	m.w	for various long narrow things	
口	*kǒu*	m.w/n	for family members; mouth	
这儿	*zhèr*	l.w	here	
有点儿	*yǒudiǎnr*	adv	somewhat; a bit	
两	*liǎng*	num	two (use in front of a measure word)	
和	*hé*	conj	and	

句型　　Speech Patterns

S	ADV	ADV	ADJ
医生		很	累。
我		有点儿	渴。
我们	都	很	饿。

S		ADJ	吗
你		饿	吗？
你们		渴	吗？
李小姐		饿	吗？

S	TW	ADV	ADV	ADJ
我			不	饿。
我	今天		不	忙。
他们		都	不	渴。

S		ADJ	不	ADJ
你们		忙	不	忙？
他的中文		好	不	好？
北京烤鸭		贵	不	贵？

Unlike in English, most Chinese adjectives can be used as verbs to indicate a state (also termed as stative verbs). In a statement, such adjectives would always be modified by an adverb of degree.

As shown before, it is easy to change a statement into a question by simply adding 吗 at the end.

The negative form of the S - Adj sentence is just to add 不 before the Adj (SV).

Also, you may use 不 to make up an affirmative-negative question.

补充词汇　　Additional Vocabulary

wàijiāoguān	外交官	diplomat	piányi	便宜	cheap
mìshu	秘书	secretary	gāoxìng	高兴	glad
zhíyuán	职员	office worker	shūfu	舒服	comfortable
hùshi	护士	nurse	piàoliang	漂亮	beautiful
jǐngchá	警察	police	nánkàn	难看	ugly; bad (book, film)
sī jī	司机	driver	nánchī	难吃	taste bad (food)

对话 1   **Dialogue One**

李：小王，你家有几口人？

王：我家有四口人，爸爸、妈妈、哥哥和我。

李：你哥哥也是学生吗？

王：不，他是医生。我爸爸、妈妈也是医生。

李：你哥哥的女朋友也是医生吧？

王：他还没有女朋友呢。你爸爸妈妈做什么工作？

李：我爸爸是商人，我妈妈是作家。

王：你们家只有三口人吗？

李：不，我还有一个姐姐，她是律师。

王：你家有狗吗？

李：我家没有狗，我妈不喜欢狗，她喜欢猫。我家有两只猫。

对话 2   **DialogueTwo**

李：小王，你今天忙不忙？

王：忙，我今天很忙。你呢？

李：我不很忙。你累不累？

王：我不累，可是我有点儿渴。

李：喝点儿茶吧，我这儿有茶。

王：好，我喝一点儿。

李：你饿不饿？我这儿还有吃的。

王：我不饿。谢谢。

语法注释　　　　Grammar Notes

1. **他还没有女朋友呢** - 还没有…呢 means "not…yet" as a contrastive response to the question that assumed that the elder brother already has a girlfriend.

2. **两只猫** - When number "two" is used together with a measure word, 两 is normally used instead of 二. For example: 两杯茶，两瓶酒，两个人.

3. **吃的** - The element after 的 is usually understood in the context and thus could be omitted in this case. This construction of verb + 的 is very common in spoken Chinese, such as 我很渴，你有没有喝的？

4. **我这儿有茶** - 这儿 means "here" and as a location word. Thus it precedes the relevant verb.

5. **有点儿／一点儿** - 有点儿 means "somewhat" or "a little bit", it is used as adverbial phrase to modify adjectives while 一点儿 means "a bit", it modifies nouns. For example, 我有点儿饿，我想吃（一）点儿饭。

文化知识 - Cultural Note

中国的家庭　　Size of Chinese Family

Due to the implementation of the family planning policy since the mid-1970s, the average size of the Chinese family in PR China has become much smaller compared to the traditional extended family. One child per couple is very common in the urban areas, though in rural areas, especially those economically underdeveloped areas a similar couple may have two or three children. Generally speaking, the decrease in the number of people in Chinese family is evident. As a result, many of the kinship terminologies depicting the complicated relationship in a family are rarely used nowadays.

练习 Exercises

口语练习 Speaking Practice

1. Work in pairs to introduce to each other the following details of some members of your family or your friends or colleagues.

Relationship	Name	Job	Age	Hobbies	Other information

2. Work in small groups or in the whole class to introduce what you have gathered from your language partner in the first exercise.

听力练习 Listening Practice

1. Listen and repeat, pay attention to the tone of the first syllable in each word.

烤鸭	*kǎoyā*	很多	*hěnduō*	老师	*lǎoshī*
网球	*wǎngqiú*	打球	*dǎqiú*	想学	*xiǎngxué*
很好	*hěnhǎo*	想你	*xiǎngnǐ*	法语	*fǎyǔ*
炒饭	*chǎofàn*	炒菜	*chǎocài*	几岁	*jǐsuì*
晚上	*wǎngshang*	姐姐	*jiějie*	喜欢	*xǐhuan*

2. Listen to the short dialogues and choose the right answer for each question.

1) a. 六口   b. 五口   c. 四口

2) a. 老师   b. 作家   c. 医生

3) a. 渴   b. 忙   c. 饿

4)　　a. 弟弟　　　　　　b. 妹妹　　　　　c. 哥哥

5)　　a. 一只　　　　　　b. 三只　　　　　c. 没有

6)　　a. 中医医生　　　　b. 中学老师　　　c. 中学生

语法练习　Grammar Practice

1. Choose the correct word in A, B or C to complete each of the following sentences.

1)　　我 _____ 累。

　　　a. 一点儿　　　b. 没　　　　　c. 不

2)　　他有 _____ 妹妹。

　　　a. 两个　　　　b. 二个　　　　c. 二口

3)　　他们 _____ 饿。

　　　a. 一点儿　　　b. 有点儿　　　c. 有

4)　　我女朋友有一 _____ 猫。

　　　a. 条　　　　　b. 只　　　　　c. 口

5)　　你爸爸 _____ 什么工作？

　　　a. 是　　　　　b. 做　　　　　c. 应该

6)　　我有姐姐 _____ 妹妹，可是我没有哥哥。

　　　a. 都　　　　　b. 也　　　　　c. 和

2. Fill in the blank with an appropriate word to complete each sentence.

1)　　他姐姐 _____ 中学老师。

2)　　医生今天不 _____ 忙。

3)　　我很累，_____ 很渴。

4)　　小李的哥哥 _____ 有女朋友。

5)　　你 _____ 什么工作？

6)　　李明的妈妈有两条 _____ 。

认读练习　Matching up

Please follow the example and link up each of the Chinese words with its corresponding pinyin and meaning in English.

说法 —————	*shuōfa*	idea
想法	*kělè*	boy student
做法	*zuòyè*	way of saying
国家	*zuòfa*	good friend
好友	*xiǎngfa*	way of doing
可乐	*guójiā*	girl student
男生	*gōngrén*	state, country
女生	*hǎoyǒu*	homework
作业	*nánshēng*	worker
工人	*nǚshēng*	coke

翻译练习　Translation

Say the following sentences in Chinese first, and then write them out in characters.

1. What do your parents do?
2. Mrs. Wang has two cats and three dogs.
3. I'm a bit busy today.
4. There are 5 people in his family.
5. I'm neither hungry nor thirsty.
6. Li Xiaoying is 24 years old. She has two elder sisters, one younger brother, and three younger sisters.

阅读　Reading

我家有几口人？

我叫方明英，今年二十岁。我家有爸爸、妈妈、姐姐、妹妹和我。

我爸爸是英国人，我妈妈是中国人，他们都是大学老师。我爸爸是英文老师，我妈妈是中文老师。我姐姐是律师，她的男朋友是作家，他是俄国 (Éguó - Russia) 人，可是他会说英语、法语和一点儿汉语，他很喜欢学外语。我妹妹今年八岁，是个小学生。我们家还有一条狗和两只猫。我妹妹说："我们家应该是九口人。"你说我们家有几口人？

Please answer the following questions based on the information in the above text.
1. What do Fang Mingying's parents do?
2. Does she have any brothers and sisters?
3. Where is her elder sister's boy friend from?
4. Do they have any pets at home?
5. What is your answer to the question at the end of the passage?

汉字知识 Chinese Characters

Radicals 偏旁部首

The Chinese word for radical is 偏旁部首 *(piānpáng bùshǒu)* and radicals play a very important role in compound characters. Being able to recognize these radicals helps in the learning and understanding of new characters, including looking up new characters in dictionaries. There are 214 radicals, but the most frequently used ones are said to be between 40-50.

偏旁 refers to the **side radicals**, which could be either semantic or phonetic in nature and usually take the left or the right position in compound characters. The following table lists four common **side semantic radicals** together with compounds in which they each occur.

Semantic radical	Meaning	Examples		
火	fire	炒	烧	烤
氵	water	渴	游	泳
女	women	姐	妈	妹
口	mouth	吧	吃	喝

汉字笔顺 Stroke Order

口	丨	冂	口							
工	一	丁	工							
作	丿	亻	亻	亻	竹	作	作			
女	乀	乆	女							
男	丶	冂	日	田	田	田	男	男		
爸	丶	八	父	父	谷	爷	爸	爸		
妈	乁	乆	女	妈	妈	妈				
和	一	二	千	手	禾	禾	和	和		
两	一	冂	币	丙	丙	两	两			
条	丿	夂	冬	冬	条	条	条			
朋	丿	刀	月	月	刖	朋	朋	朋		
友	一	ナ	方	友						
家	丶	宀	宀	宀	宁	宁	穷	家	家	家
哥	一	丆	币	苛	可	亚	哥	哥	哥	哥
忙	丶	忄	忄	忙	忙	忙				
饿	丿	𠂉	饣	饣	饣	饣	饳	饿	饿	
渴	丶	冫	氵	沪	沪	沪	渇	渴	渴	渴
累	丶	冂	日	田	田	罒	罗	累	累	累
猫	丿	犭	犭	犭	犷	犷	猫	猫	猫	猫
狗	丿	犭	犭	犭	狗	狗	狗	狗		
律	丿	彳	彳	彳	律	律	律	律	律	
商	丶	亠	产	产	产	商	商	商	商	商

写字练习   **Character Writing Exercise**

Can you recognise these characters? Test yourself if you are able to write the pinyin and English meaning on top of each character. Then copy each character following its stroke order on the opposite page. Try to have a feel of the structure of the character when copying, especially those consisting of two or three components.

口						工					
朋						友					
女						两					
男						累					
爸						家					
商						哥					
忙						作					
和						条					
狗						猫					
妈						饿					
律						渴					

第九课　北京夏天比伦敦热

Learning objectives

Talk about weather in different seasons

Compare weather in different places

Make a comparison and give a suggestion

生词　　New Words

下雨	*xiàyǔ*	v-o	rain	下 fall; get off　雨 rain
下雪	*xiàxuě*	v-o	snow	雪 snow
比	*bǐ*	v/prep	compare; compared with	
冷	*lěng*	adj	cold	
热	*rè*	adj	hot	
暖和	*nuǎnhuo*	adj	warm	暖 warm
漂亮	*piàoliang*	adj	pretty	漂 * smart　亮 *liàng* bright, shiny
高	*gāo*	adj	tall (person or building), high	
胖	*pàng*	adj	stout; fat	
瘦	*shòu*	adj	thin (a person)	
少	*shǎo*	adj	few; little	
春天	*chūntiān*	n	spring	春 spring
夏天	*xiàtiān*	n	summer	夏 summer
秋天	*qiūtiān*	n	autumn	秋 autumn
冬天	*dōngtiān*	n	winter	冬 winter
天气	*tiānqì*	n	weather	气 air; breath
常常	*chángcháng*	adv	often	常 often
一样	*yīyàng*	adj/adv	the same	样 * (m.w/n) type; manner
怎么样	*zěnmeyàng*	q.w	how is it?	怎 * how; why
多了	*duōle*		much more	了 (pt) (part of a complement)

句型   **Speech Patterns**

A	比	B	ADJ
中国	比	英国	大。
北京夏天	比	伦敦（夏天）	热。
他	比	我	高。

Chinese comparison follows a simple formula "A 比 B + Adj" as shown on the left.

A	比	B	ADJ	COMP
北京	比	伦敦	热	多了。
他弟弟	比	他	瘦	一点儿。
我哥哥	比	我	大	一岁。

Unlike in English the Chinese adverbial modifier of degree (such as "much" and "a bit") appears as a complement after the adj it modifies.

A	没（有）	B	ADJ
我哥哥	没（有）	我	高。
伦敦夏天	没（有）	北京（夏天）	热。
英国	没（有）	法国	大。

The negative form of the comparison is 没有. In spoken Chinese, 有 is often omitted.

A	和	B	一样	ADJ
她	和	我	一样	大。
他哥哥	和	他	一样	高。
北京夏天	和	上海	一样	热。

The formula on the left is used when one wants to express the idea that the two compared are the same.

补充词汇   **Additional Vocabulary**

liángkuai	凉快	cool	*ǎi*	矮	short (height)
mēnrè	闷热	muggy, close	*fù/yǒuqián*	富 / 有钱	rich
gānzào	干燥	dry	*qióng/méiqián*	穷 / 没钱	poor
cháoshī	潮湿	damp, humid	*yǒuyòng*	有用	useful
qīng	轻	light (weight)	*yuǎn*	远	far
zhòng	重	heavy (weight)	*jìn*	近	near, close

◆ 对话 1　　**Dialogue One**

方：小王，你女朋友很漂亮！

王：谢谢。你有没有女朋友？

方：有，可是她没你女朋友漂亮。

王：她胖不胖？

王：不胖，她很瘦。比你女朋友瘦多了。

方：瘦好，胖不好。

王：太瘦也不好。

方：你女朋友比你小吧？

王：对，她比我小三岁。

◆ 对话 2　　**Dialogue Two**

李：小王，北京的天气怎么样？

王：夏天很热，冬天很冷。

李：北京夏天比伦敦热吗？

王：比伦敦热多了！

李：北京的春天怎么样？

王：春天很好，很暖和。

李：常常下雨吗？

王：春天雨很少，可是夏天雨很多。

李：北京冬天下不下雨？

王：冬天不下雨，冬天下雪。

李：我喜欢下雪天。北京的秋天怎么样？

王：秋天很好，不冷不热。

语法注释　Grammar Notes

1. 北京夏天比伦敦夏天热 - 夏天 after 伦敦 is usually omitted as it is clear from the context. 北京夏天很热 means pretty much the same thing as 北京的夏天很热 though their sentence structures are different. There will be more detailed discussion later.

2. 北京夏天比伦敦热多了 - 了 is a particle used in a number of ways in Chinese. Here it goes together with the word 多 to form the expression 多了 meaning "much more" to provide more information on the 热 preceding it.

3. 她没你女朋友漂亮 - The negative form for a comparison sentence with 比 is " A 没有 B + Adj " as shown above. But there is a " A 不比 B + Adj " sentence structure which means that A and B are not much different. This structure is rarely used to start a sentence, but used as a response to retort an argument. For an example:

    1)   我没有小李高。   I am not as tall as Xiao Li.

    2)   a: 你太太比你高。   Your wife is taller than you.

            b: 她不比我高。   She is not taller than I am.

文化知识 - Cultural Note

中文里的"胖"字　The Chinese Word 胖

Traditionally, the word has been used as a compliment to suggest that someone looks very healthy and is not short of food. In a country where there are many mouths to feed, it has always been a blessing if one could afford to put on some weight. As time moves on, Chinese concept of health and well being changes too. Nowadays, while the word is still very much used by some people, particularly parents in a commendatory way, the younger generation, especially young women are very sensitive to the word, often taking it as a derogatory term, just as in the West.

练习　Exercises

口语练习　Speaking Practice

1. Work in pairs and talk about the weather in London and in places you know.

2. Work in pairs or small groups to describe someone (friends, family members) or something (food, drink). For example:

I am tall.

I am taller than my elder brother.

I am a bit taller than my elder brother.

I am much taller than my elder brother.

I am not as tall as my elder brother.

听力练习　Listening Practice

1. Listen and repeat, pay attention to the neutral tone in each word.

1)	先生 *xiānsheng*	医生 *yīsheng*	他们 *tāmen*	商人 *shāngren*
2)	什么 *shénme*	名字 *míngzi*	学生 *xuésheng*	朋友 *péngyou*
3)	怎么 *zěnme*	我们 *wǒmen*	暖和 *nuǎnhuo*	姐姐 *jiějie*
4)	谢谢 *xièxie*	认识 *rènshi*	漂亮 *piàoliang*	太太 *tàitai*

2. Listen to the short dialogues and choose the right answer for each question.

1)　a. 我高　　　b. 我弟弟高　　　c. 我们一样高

2)　a. 北京冷　　　b. 伦敦冷　　　c. 北京暖和

3)　a. 她姐姐高　　　b. 她高　　　c. 她们一样高

4)　a. 冬天　　　b. 春天　　　c. 夏天

5)　a. 下雨天　　　b. 热天　　　c. 下雪天

6)　a. 法国　　　b. 英国　　　c. 北京

语法练习　Grammar Practice

1. Choose the correct word in A, B or C to complete each of the following sentences.

1) 她 _____ 她姐姐一样漂亮。

　　a. 没有　　　　b. 比　　　　c. 和

2) 我女朋友 _____ 我高一点儿。

　　a. 没有　　　　b. 比　　　　c. 和

3) 我弟弟 _____ 我爸爸胖。

　　a. 没有　　　　b. 和　　　　c. 一样

4) 北京夏天比伦敦热 _____ 了。

　　a. 不多　　　　b. 多　　　　c. 很多

5) 伦敦的秋天和北京的秋天 _____ 好，不冷不热。

　　a. 一点儿　　　b. 多　　　　c. 一样

6) 我哥哥比我姐姐 _____ 。

　　a. 大两岁　　　b. 两岁大　　　c. 一样大

2. Use the given information to make up sentences using comparison.

	A	B	Adj
1)	夏天	春天	热
2)	中国	法国	大
3)	北京冬天	伦敦冬天	冷
4)	伦敦春天	伦敦冬天	漂亮
5)	中国菜	英国菜	好吃
6)	我	我哥哥	小

认读练习 Matching up

Please follow the example and link up each of the Chinese words with its corresponding pinyin and meaning in English.

大小	——— dàxiǎo	heating
大家	xiǎoshuō	queen (head of state)
生气	nuǎnqì	size
暖气	nǚwáng	calligraphy
春雨	jiāshū	stingy
女王	xiǎoqì	letter (from) home
小气	shēngqì	angry
小说	chūnyǔ	spring rain
书法	dàjiā	novel
家书	shūfǎ	all of us

翻译练习 Translation

Say the following sentences in Chinese first, and then write them out in characters.

1. China is larger than Britain.
2. I like spring very much. It is neither cold nor hot.
3. I am as tall as my boyfriend.
4. Our dog is not as big as yours.
5. Roast duck is more expensive than stir-fried beef with green vegetables.
6. What is the weather like in London in winter? London is much warmer than Beijing in winter.

阅读 Reading

<h3 style="text-align:center">我姐姐和北京的天气</h3>

我姐姐叫李小英，她是律师，她在 (zài - in) 北京工作。她说她很喜欢北京的冬天。北京的冬天很冷，常常下雪。伦敦的冬天比北京暖和，可是常

常下雨，我和我姐姐都不喜欢下雨天，我们喜欢下雪天。北京的夏天很热，比伦敦热多了。我姐姐有点儿胖，她不喜欢太热的天气，所以 (suǒyǐ - so) 她不太喜欢北京的夏天。北京的春天和秋天很好，不冷不热，也不常常下雨。我姐姐说，春天的北京很漂亮，我想明年春天去 (qù - go) 北京看我姐姐，也看看 (have a look) 漂亮的北京。

Please answer the following questions based on the information in the above text.

1. Where is Li Xiaoying working and what kind of job is she doing?
2. What is the weather like in Beijing in winter?
3. Why doesn't Li Xiaoying like Beijing's summer?
4. How is the weather in London as compared to Beijing in summer?
5. What is the narrator going to do next spring and why?

汉字知识　Chinese Characters

Phonetic Components　声旁

Though there is no hard rule in Chinese on how a sound is determined as alphabetic languages would, many independent characters could provide some clue on the pronunciation of the semantic-phonetic compounds they help to form. They usually retain finals (vowels), which seem to be consistent while initials may change depending on what semantic radicals they are combined with. One example is given in the table below.

Semantic radical		Phonetic component	Compound	Pinyin	Meaning
rain	雨		雹	*báo*	hail
food	饣		饱	*bǎo*	full (not hungry)
hand	扌	包 *bāo* (bag)	抱	*bào*	take in arms
mouth	口		咆	*páo*	shout, roar
foot	足		跑	*pǎo*	run
water	氵		泡	*pào*	soak, marinate

汉字笔顺　Stroke Order

了	㇋	了										
下	一	丁	下									
少	丨	小	小	少								
气	丿	㇒	乞	气								
比	一	上	上	比								
高	、	亠	亠	亠	古	户	高	高	高	高		
怎	丿	乍	乍	乍	乍	乍	怎	怎	怎			
样	一	十	才	木	术	栏	栏	栏	栏	样		
雨	一	厂	厅	币	币	雨	雨	雨				
雪	一	厂	一	币	雨	雫	雫	雪	雪	雪	雪	
冷	、	丿	冫	冸	冷	冷	冷					
热	一	十	扌	扚	执	执	执	热	热	热		
常	丶	丷	丷	兴	兴	兴	常	常	常	常	常	
春	一	二	三	声	夫	表	春	春	春			
夏	一	丆	丁	百	百	百	百	頁	夏	夏		
秋	丿	二	千	禾	禾	禾	秋	秋	秋			
冬	丿	夂	夂	冬	冬	冬						
暖	日	旷	旷	旷	旷	旷	暖	暖	暖	暖		
漂	、	氵	汇	沪	沪	湮	湮	湮	漂	漂	漂	
亮	、	亠	亠	古	古	户	亮	亮	亮			
胖	丿	月	月	月	月	肸	肸	肸	胖			
瘦	、	亠	广	广	疒	疒	疒	疒	疸	疸	疸	瘦

写字练习　**Character Writing Exercise**

Can you recognise these characters? Test yourself if you are able to write the pinyin and English meaning on top of each character. Then copy each character following its stroke order on the opposite page. Try to have a feel of the structure of the character when copying, especially those consisting of two or three components.

了						下					
少						气					
比						冬					
雨						雪					
亮						高					
春						暖					
热						瘦					
常						冷					
怎						样					
胖						秋					
夏						漂					

第十课　你怎么去商店？

Learning objectives

Talk about going somewhere to do something

Talk about coming to do something

Express how to go/come somewhere

生词　　　　New Words

去	qù	v	go (to)			
来	lái	v	come (opposite direction of 去)			
还书	huán shū	v-o	return books	还 return		
骑	qí	v	ride (bicycle, horse etc)			
坐	zuò	v	sit			
回家	huíjiā	v-o	go back home	回 go back, return		
开车	kāichē	v-o	drive	开 drive; open	车 vehicle	
打的	dǎdī	v-o	take a taxi (的 is read as *dī* here for taxi)			
走路	zǒulù	v-o	walk	走 walk	路 road	
上班	shàngbān	v-o	go to work	班 shift		
自行车	zìxíngchē	n	bicycle	自 self	行 walk	
火车	huǒchē	n	locomotive, train	火 fire		
公共	gōnggòng	adj	public	公 public	共 common	
汽车	qìchē	n	vehicle, car	汽 steam		
公共汽车	gōnggòng qìchē	n	bus			
图书馆	túshūguǎn	n	library	图 map; picture	馆 building	
东方	dōngfāng	n	the east	东 east		
地铁	dìtiě	n	underground train	铁 iron		
商店	shāngdiàn	n	shop	店 shop		
学院	xuéyuàn	n	college	院 compound; courtyard		
商学院	shāngxuéyuàn	n	business school/college			
哪儿	nǎr	q.w	where			
怎么	zěnme	q.w	how			

句型　Speech Patterns

S	来 / 去	Place
他们	来	伦敦。
你	去	哪儿?
我	去	商店。

Please note the position of the question word when asking about the place, and the way in which the answer is given.

S	TW	来 / 去	Place
我	明天	去	中国。
我们	明年	去	北京。
她	今晚	来	我家。

A time word always goes before the verb, as said before.

S	TW	来 / 去	Place	V	O
我	明天	去	图书馆	还	书。
他	明年	去	北京	学	汉语。
她	天天	来	我家	看	我。

The pattern (go somewhere to do something) is nearly the same as in English except for the position of the time word.

S	TW	V	O	来 / 去	Place
我	天天	坐	地铁	去	学院。
她	明天	骑	车	去	商店。
他	今晚	开	车	来	伦敦。

The verbal phrases before 去 / 来 seem to be like English prepositional phrases, and such verbs are termed co-verbs in some textbooks as they "help" to express the manner of the main action verb.

补充词汇　Additional Vocabulary

zuò chē	坐车	by vehicle	xiàwǔ	下午	afternoon
zuò chūzūchē	坐出租车	by taxi	jiè shū	借书	borrow books
zuò fēijī	坐飞机	by plane	kāihuì	开会	have/attend a meeting
zuò chuán	坐船	by boat/ship	mǎi dōngxi	买东西	shopping
shàngwǔ	上午	morning	chūchāi	出差	go on a business trip
zhōngwǔ	中午	noon	dùjià	度假	go on a holiday

对话 1　　Dialogue One

王：小李，你去哪儿？

李：我去商店。

王：你去哪家商店？

李：我去那家东方商店。你去哪儿？

王：我去图书馆。

李：今天星期六，你去图书馆做什么？

王：我去图书馆还书。

李：你怎么去？我有自行车，你骑我的车去吧。

王：谢谢，我喜欢走路，我还是走路去吧。

对话 2　　Dialogue Two

李：老王，你回家吗？

王：不，我先去商学院再回家。

李：你去商学院做什么？

王：我去看一个朋友。他是那儿的老师。

李：明天没有地铁，你怎么来上班？

王：我坐火车来。你呢？

李：我想坐公共汽车来。

王：你怎么不打的来，打的比坐公共汽车快多了。

李：可是也贵多了。

王：对。你不是有汽车吗？为什么不开车来？

李：因为我还不会开车。

语法注释　Grammar Notes

1. **我先去商学院再回家** - 再 is used here before the verb to refer to a deferred action, or "then" rather than the meaning of "again" as in 再见. For example:

　1)　今天很冷，我明天再去。

　2)　我们先去北京，再去东京。

2. **我还是走路去吧** - 还是⋯吧 is a construction, meaning "it would be better if…" or "you'd better…" when the subject is the second person as a kind of suggestion. For instance:

　1)　你还是先吃饭吧。

　2)　你还是坐汽车去吧。

文化知识 - Cultural Note

中国的出租车　The Chinese Taxi

The formal term for taxis in Chinese is called 出租车 (chūzūchē). While it is right to say 我天天坐出租车去商学院 (I go to work by taxi everyday), many Chinese nowadays would use the more colloquial term 打的, an expression taken from Cantonese. So for the same sentence above you are more likely to hear Chinese say 我天天打的去商学院. In fact there are many expressions in contemporary Chinese taken from other languages or dialects, which shows how Chinese is interacting with other languages.

练习 Exercises

口语练习 Speaking Practice

Work in pairs to talk about your one-week plan. The following is an example:

A: 星期一你去哪儿？

B: 星期一我先去医院看朋友，再去大学。

A: 你怎么去？

B: 坐地铁去。

Time	Transport	Place 1	Purpose	Place 2
星期一				
星期二				
星期三				
星期四				
星期五				
星期六				
星期天				

听力练习 Listening Practice

1. Listen and repeat, pay attention to the "r" ending.

1) *nǎr*   你去哪儿？

2) *zhèr*   这儿东西贵不贵？

3) *yīdiǎnr*   我会说一点儿中文。

4) *yǒudiǎnr*   今天有点儿冷？

5) *fànguǎnr*   我不喜欢那家饭馆儿。

2. Listen to the short dialogues and choose the right answer for each question.

1) a. 图书馆   b. 商店   c. 商学院

2) a. 坐地铁   b. 骑车   c. 开车

3) a. 还书   b. 看电视   c. 看朋友
4) a. 图书馆   b. 商学院   c. 回家
5) a. 不喜欢骑车   b. 没有自行车   c. 不会骑车
6) a. 坐公共汽车快 b. 坐火车贵   c. 没有火车

语法练习　Grammar Practice

1. Choose the correct word in A, B or C to complete each of the following sentences.

1) 她们 _____ 地铁去商店。
    a. 骑   b. 坐   c. 有

2) 我明天上午去图书馆 _____ 。
    a. 还书   b. 喝茶   c. 吃饭

3) 你今天骑车 _____ 家吗？
    a. 去   b. 上   c. 回

4) 我们 _____ 路上班吧。
    a. 走   b. 坐   c. 骑

5) 你们 _____ 去北京？
    a. 什么   b. 来   c. 怎么

6) 我星期三不忙，你星期三 _____ 我家吧。
    a. 去   b. 来   c. 走

2. Use appropriate question words to ask questions about the underlined parts.

1) <u>他</u>明天开车去商学院看朋友。
2) 他<u>明天</u>开车去商学院看朋友。
3) 他明天<u>开车</u>去商学院看朋友。
4) 他明天开车去<u>商学院</u>看朋友。
5) 他明天开车去商学院<u>看朋友</u>。
6) 他明天开车去商学院看<u>朋友</u>。

认读练习　Matching up

Please follow the example and link up each of the Chinese words with its corresponding pinyin and meaning in English.

地图	*shūdiàn*	tram, trolley
书店	*fǎxuéyuàn*	pedestrian
行人	*wàiyǔ xuéyuàn*	hospital
回国	*fàndiàn*	map
电车	*yīyuàn*	restaurant, hotel
医院	*xíngrén*	medical school
医学院	*huíguó*	bookshop
饭店	*dìtú*	law school
法学院	*diànchē*	go back to the country
外语学院	*yīxuéyuàn*	foreign language institute

翻译练习　Translation

Say the following sentences in Chinese first, and then write them out in characters.

1. I shall not drive to the school tomorrow.
2. Where are you going? I am going to the bookshop to buy books.
3. Mr Li will take the Tube home today.
4. He goes to the library to read every day.
5. My mother can't ride a bike, she goes to work by bus every day.
6. Wang Ming won't come to work tomorrow. He is going to Beijing this evening.

阅读　Reading

我喜欢骑车去上班

天天早上，很多人开车或 (*huò* - or) 坐车去上班。你们都怎么去上班呢？

春夏秋冬，我差不多 (*chàbudūo* - nearly) 天天都骑自行车去上班。伦敦有地铁，也有很多公共汽车，可是我不喜欢坐地铁。伦敦坐地铁的人很多，夏天坐地铁很热，<u>再说</u> (besides)，坐地铁也很贵。我也不喜欢坐伦敦的公共汽车，伦敦的<u>路上行人</u> (pedestrians) 和汽车太多，骑车常常比坐公共汽车快。今天是星期六，我不上班。我要骑车去我女朋友家，看她爸爸妈妈，晚上我们一起去看电影。

Please answer the following questions based on the information in the above text.

1. According to the reading, how does the person go to work every day?
2. Why doesn't the person like the underground?
3. What does the person think about the buses?
4. What does he plan to do today?
5. How do you go to work?

汉字知识　Chinese Characters

Simplified and Complicated form Chinese Characters
简繁体汉字

There are two forms of Chinese characters in use, simplified characters (简体字 - *jiǎntǐzì*) and complicated character (繁体字 - *fántǐzì*). The simplified characters became official in the mid-1950s in PR China and are now widely accepted and used abroad.

Compared with complicated characters, simplified characters have a reduced number of strokes for many characters. The simplification of some 2000 characters is based upon a number of principles in line with the characteristics of Chinese characters and the actual use of those characters in daily life. The table below lists some characters with both forms and their number of strokes.

Simplified characters	学	医	后	尘	书
No of strokes	8	7	6	6	4
English	study	medical	behind	dust	book
Pinyin	*xué*	*yī*	*hòu*	*chén*	*shū*
Complicated characters	學	醫	後	塵	書
No of strokes	16	18	9	14	10

汉字笔顺　Stroke Order

开	一	二	于	开								
去	一	十	土	去	去							
来	一	一	ㄎ	立	平	来	来					
回	丨	冂	冋	回	回	回						
火	丶	⺍	少	火								
公	丿	八	公	公								
共	一	十	卅	共	共	共						
汽	丶	丶	氵	沪	汽	汽	汽					
车	一	七	二	车								
自	丿	亻	白	白	自	自						
行	丿	彳	彳	彳	行	行						
东	一	七	东	东	东							
坐	丿	人	从	从	丛	坐	坐					
店	丶	二	广	广	庄	庄	店	店				
走	一	十	土	卡	卡	走	走					
路	丶	口	口	甲	甲	呈	足	趵	趵	政	趵	路	路
院	阝	阝	阝	阝	阼	陀	陀	阼	院			
铁	丿	广	车	车	钅	钊	钎	钌	铁	铁		
班	一	二	干	王	王	到	玒	玨	班	班		
图	丨	冂	冂	冈	冈	冈	图	图				
馆	丿	亇	亇	亇	饣	饣	馆	馆	馆	馆		
骑	乛	马	马	马	马	骈	骈	骑	骑	骑		

写字练习　Character Writing Exercise

Can you recognise these characters? Test yourself if you are able to write the pinyin and English meaning on top of each character. Then copy each character following its stroke order on the opposite page. Try to have a feel of the structure of the character when copying, especially those consisting of two or three components.

开					车				
火					去				
来					回				
东					图				
坐					走				
公					共				
自					行				
汽					店				
院					馆				
铁					班				
骑					路				

Abbreviations of Grammatical Terms

adj	adjective
adv	adverb
comp	complement
conj	conjunction
id	idiomatic expression
int	interjection
l.w	location word
m.v	modal verb
m.w	measure word
n	noun
num	number
o	object
pt	particle
p.n	proper name
pron	pronoun
prep	preposition
q.w	question word
s	subject
t.w	time word
v	verb
v-c	verb-complement
v-o	verb -object

✧ Chinese characters noted with * are usually not used on their own, but as a component part to form a word.

Keys to the Exercises

Lesson One

听力练习 - Listening Practice

1. Listen and choose the phrase you have heard in each group.

  1) c;   2) a;   3) a;   4) c;   5) c;   6) b

认读练习 - Matching up

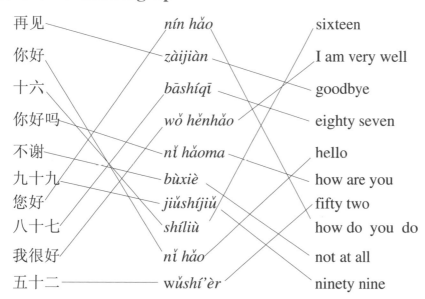

再见	*nín hǎo*	sixteen
你好	*zàijiàn*	I am very well
十六	*bāshíqī*	goodbye
你好吗	*wǒ hěnhǎo*	eighty seven
不谢	*nǐ hǎoma*	hello
九十九	*bùxiè*	how are you
您好	*jiǔshíjiǔ*	fifty two
八十七	*shíliù*	how do you do
我很好	*nǐ hǎo*	not at all
五十二	*wǔshí'èr*	ninety nine

Lesson Two

拼音练习 - Pinyin Practice

3. Listen and circle the pinyin you have heard in each group.

  1) *jiāo*   2) *nián*   3) *cī*   4) *chāng*

  5) *kǎo*   6) *nán*   7) *shī*   8) *yuè*

听力练习 - Listening Practice

Listen to the short dialogues and mark if each of the following sentences is true (T) or false (F).

  1. T;   2. F;   3. F;   4. T;   5. F;   6. F

语法练习 - Grammar Practice

1. Turn the following sentences into negative and general question forms.

  1) a. 我不叫李小英。   b. 你叫李小英吗？

  2) a. 你也不姓王。   b. 你也姓王吗？

  3) a. 他不叫方国伦。   b. 他叫方国伦吗？

  4) a. 他不叫王京。   b. 他叫王京吗？

  5) a. 她不姓方。   b. 她姓方吗？

  6) a. 她不叫李国英。   b. 她叫李国英吗？

2. Complete the following dialogues by filling in the blanks with appropriate words given below.

  1) A. 您贵**姓**？   2) A. 你叫**什么**名字？

  3) B. **不**，她不姓王。   4) B. 我**也**姓李。

  5) A. 我叫方国伦，你**呢**？   6) B. **对**，他叫王京。

认读练习 - Matching up

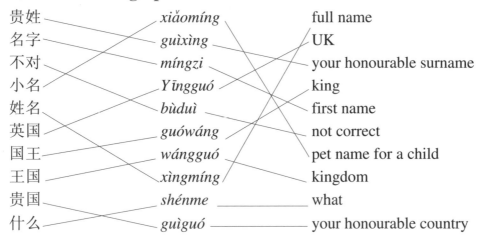

贵姓	*xiǎomíng*	full name
名字	*guìxìng*	UK
不对	*míngzi*	your honourable surname
小名	*Yīngguó*	king
姓名	*bùduì*	first name
英国	*guówáng*	not correct
国王	*wángguó*	pet name for a child
王国	*xìngmíng*	kingdom
贵国	*shénme*	what
什么	*guìguó*	your honourable country

翻译练习 - Translation

  1. 您贵姓？

  2. 我叫王英，你叫什么（名字）？

  3. 他叫什么（名字）？

  4. 她也姓李。

  5. 你叫方国伦吗？不，我不叫方国伦。

  6. 你叫什么名字？我叫方英。

Lesson Three

拼音练习 - Pinyin Practice

3. Listen and circle the pinyin you have heard in each group

  1) *shāng*   2) *zǒu*   3) *chù*   4) *xiàn*

  5) *jué*   6) *lǜ*   7) *lóng*   8) *luǎn*

听力练习 - Listening Practice

Listen to the short dialogues and mark if each of the following sentences is true (T) or false (F).

  1. F;   2. T;   3. F;   4. F;   5. F;   6. F

语法练习 - Grammar Practice

1.Turn the following sentences into choice questions (CQ) or special questions (SQ).

  1) 他叫什么(名字)?   2) 你是不是英国人?

  3) 王小姐是什么地方人?   4) 你老师是不是中国人?

  5) 那是谁?   6) 你们是不是医生?

2. Complete the following dialogues by filling in the blanks with appropriate words given below.

  1) A. 你是**哪**国人?   2) A. 他是**谁**?

  3) A. 你们是**不**是伦敦人?   4) A. 她是**什么**地方人?

  5) B. 我们不**都**是中国人。   6) B. **不是**，他是老师。

认读练习 - Matching up

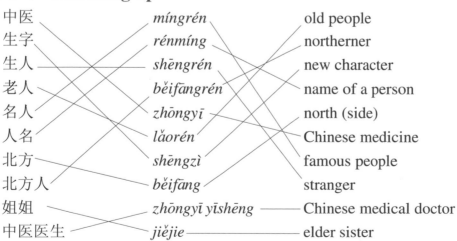

翻译练习 - Translation

1. 你是哪国人？

2. 他是谁？他就是王老师。

3. 这是方小姐，她也是北京人。

4. 那是李先生，他是医生。

5. 我们都是英国人。

6. 他们都不是医生。

Lesson Four

拼音练习 - Pinyin Practice

3. Listen and circle the pinyin you have heard in each group.

1) *qīn*　　　2) *xīn*　　　3) *róu*　　　4) *móu*

5) *niǎo*　　6) *xiǎo*　　7) *xùn*　　8) *jùn*

听力练习 - Listening Practice

Listen to the short dialogues and choose the correct answer for each question.

1. a)　十月一号　　2. c)　二月十七日　　3. c)　星期三

4. c)　中国人　　5. a)　六月二十九号　　6. c)　我弟弟的

语法练习 - Grammar Practice

1. Ask questions about the underlined parts in the following sentences.

1) 你的生日是九月几号？

2) 你妹妹今年几岁？

3) 今天(是)星期六，明天(是)星期几？

4) 明天是谁的生日？

5) 哪天是小李的生日？

6) 王老师是(中国)什么地方人？

2. Complete the following dialogues by filling in the blanks with appropriate words given below.

1. B. 我的生日是**三月六号**。　　2. A. 你弟弟**几岁**？

3. A. 明天是你**的**生日吗？　　4. A. 她**多**大？

5. B. **明天**七号。　　6. A. 今天星期**几**？

认读练习 - Matching up

年年 —— míngxīng —— elderly people
明月 —— suìyuè —— time
明星 —— zhōngniánrén —— everyone
老年人 —— míngyuè —— medium size
中年人 —— niánnián —— star
大号 —— lǎoniánrén —— middle aged people
小号 —— dàhào —— bright moon
岁月 —— rénrén —— every year
人人 —— zhōnghào —— big size
中号 —— xiǎohào —— small size

翻译练习 - Translation

1. 今天几号？
2. 今天是你的生日，生日快乐！
3. 你多大？（你几岁？）
4. 今年是 2005 年，明年是 2006 年。
5. 明天星期几？明天星期六。
6. 他是谁？他是我妹妹的老师。

Lesson Five

拼音练习 - Pinyin Practice

3. Listen and circle the pinyin you have heard in each group.

1) dìtóu   2) dàlóu   3) sàngshī   4) shǒushì
5) Chángchéng   6) chánglóng   7) jiǎnfà   8) jiǎnghuà

听力练习 - Listening Practice

Listen to the short dialogues and mark if each of the following sentences is true (T) or false (F).

1. F;   2. F;   3. T;   4. F;   5. T;   6. T

语法练习 - Grammar Practice

1. Please insert the given word in the right place in each sentence.

　　1) 英国人（都）喝英国茶吗？

　　2) 你（今天晚上）看电视吗？

　　3) 她（天天）上网。

　　4) 我们（不）学英国文学。

　　5) 他不喝中国茶，我（也）不喝中国茶。

　　6) 这是谁（的）茶？

2. Complete the following dialogues by filling in the blanks with appropriate words given below.

　　1) B. 我学**中文**。　　　　　2) A. 你晚上**都**做什么？

　　3) B. 我**写**汉字。　　　　　4) A. 你看中文书**还是**看英文书？

　　5) B. **喝**。　　　　　　　　6) A. 你晚上**上网**吗？

认读练习 - Matching up

奶牛	zhōngxué	milk cow
奶茶	rìwén	middle school
电网	nǎichá	students
日文	dàxué	university
小学	nǎiniú	tea with milk
中学	diànwǎng	primary school
大学	xuéshēng	Japanese language
学生	xiǎoxué	electricity grid
一星期	shàngxué	go to school
上学	yī xīngqī	one whole week

翻译练习 - Translation

　　1. 你学什么专业？我学英国文学。

　　2. 你星期六做什么？

　　3. 你喝茶还是喝牛奶？

　　4. 王小姐每天晚上都写汉字。

　　5. 我早上不喝中国茶。

　　6. 你晚上看书还是看电视？

Lesson Six

听力练习 - Listening Practice

2. Listen to the short statements or dialogues and mark if each of the following sentences is true (T) or false (F).

   1. T;   2. T;   3. F;   4. T;   5. T;   6. F

语法练习 - Grammar Practice

1. Match the following verbs with their objects (verbs may be used more than once).

   1) **学/说**汉语   2) **踢**足球   3) **打**网球

   4) **看**电视   5) **学/写**汉字   6) **上**网

   7) **喝**中国茶   8) **打**篮球   9) **学/说**法语

   10) **喝**牛奶   11) **看/写**中文书   12) **看**老师

2. Complete the following sentences by filling in the blanks with appropriate words given below.

   1) 我会说**一点儿**英语。
   2) 我们今天**打**网球，好吗？
   3) 她会说汉语，**可是**她不认识汉字。
   4) 你想学**踢**足球吗？
   5) 我**喜欢**上网，可是我太太不喜欢上网。
   6) 我们都**会**说英语。

认读练习 - Matching up

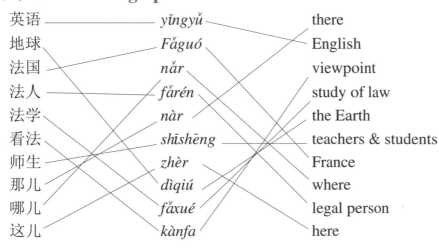

英语 —— yīngyǔ — there
地球 Fǎguó English
法国 nǎr viewpoint
法人 fǎrén study of law
法学 nàr the Earth
看法 shīshēng teachers & students
师生 zhèr France
那儿 dìqiú where
哪儿 fǎxué legal person
这儿 kànfa here

翻译练习 - Translation

1. 我的中文老师不喜欢踢足球。
2. 她不会说法语，可是她会说日语。
3. 我想学汉字。
4. 李医生会说一点儿汉语。
5. 他天天晚上上网。
6. 我想喝点儿中国茶。

Lesson Seven

听力练习 - Listening Practice

2. Listen to the short dialogues and circle the right answer accordingly.

1) c. fried rice   2) a. British beer   3) b. braised meat in sauce

4) c. Chinese tea   5) c. English books   6) b. her birthday

语法练习 - Grammar Practice

1. Choose the correct word in A, B or C to complete each of the following sentences.

1) c. 盘   2) a. 不   3) a. 杯   4) c. 要   5) b. 没   6) b. 好吃

2. Use 没 and 不 to change the following sentences into negative form.

1) 今天我们**没**有烤鸭。   2) 我**不**要日本啤酒。

3) 你**不**喜欢踢足球吗？   4) 他们**没**有中国茶。

5) 他**不**天天看电视。   6) 我们今天晚上**不**写汉字。

认读练习 - Matching up

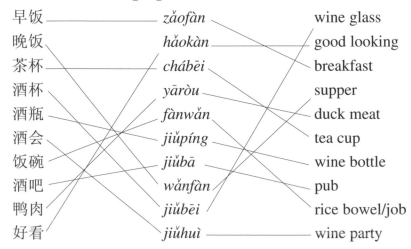

早饭	*zǎofàn*	wine glass
晚饭	*hǎokàn*	good looking
茶杯	*chábēi*	breakfast
酒杯	*yāròu*	supper
酒瓶	*fànwǎn*	duck meat
酒会	*jiǔpíng*	tea cup
饭碗	*jiǔbā*	wine bottle
酒吧	*wǎnfàn*	pub
鸭肉	*jiǔbēi*	rice bowel/job
好看	*jiǔhuì*	wine party

翻译练习 - Translation

1. 你们有中国啤酒吗？我想要一杯。
2. 今天我们没有牛肉炒青菜。
3. 明天是我的生日。我们吃中国饭好吗？
4. 我喜欢喝中国啤酒，吃北京烤鸭。
5. 我们想要四瓶法国红酒。
6. 我很喜欢吃法国饭，法国饭很好吃。

Lesson Eight

听力练习 - Listening Practice

2. Listen to the short dialogues and choose the right answer for each question.

1) a. 六口   2) b. 作家   3) a. 渴
4) c. 哥哥   5) c. 没有   6) b. 中学老师

语法练习 - Grammar Practice

1. Choose the correct word in A, B or C to complete each of the following sentences.

1) c. 不   2) a. 两个   3) b. 有点儿
4) b. 只   5) b. 做   6) c. 和

2. Fill in the blank with an appropriate word to complete each sentence.

1. 他姐姐**是**中学老师。
2. 医生今天不**很 / 太**忙。
3. 我很累，**也**很渴。
4. 小李的哥哥**也 / 没有**女朋友。
5. 你**做**什么工作？
6. 李明的妈妈有两条**狗**。

认读练习 - Matching up

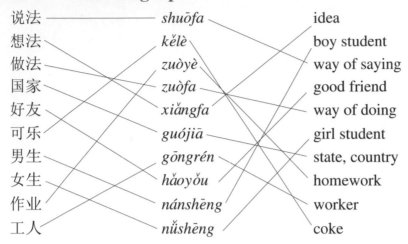

说法   *shuōfa*   idea
想法   *kělè*   boy student
做法   *zuòyè*   way of saying
国家   *zuòfa*   good friend
好友   *xiǎngfa*   way of doing
可乐   *guójiā*   girl student
男生   *gōngrén*   state, country
女生   *hǎoyǒu*   homework
作业   *nánshēng*   worker
工人   *nǚshēng*   coke

翻译练习 - Translation

1. 你爸爸妈妈（都）做什么（工作）？
2. 王太太有两只猫、（or 和）三条狗。
3. 我今天有点儿忙。
4. 他家有五口人。
5. 我不饿，也不渴。
6. 李小英 24 岁。她有两个姐姐，一个弟弟和三个妹妹。

Lesson Nine

听力练习 - Listening Practice

2. Listen to the short dialogues and choose the right answer for each question.

     1) b. 我弟弟高   2) a. 北京冷   3) a. 她姐姐高
     4) c. 夏天   5) c. 下雪天   6) a. 法国

语法练习 - Grammar Practice

1. Choose the correct word in A, B or C to complete each of the following sentences.

     1) c. 和   2) b. 比   3) a. 没有
     4) b. 多   5) c. 一样   6) a. 大两岁

2. Use the given information to make up sentences using comparison.

     1) 夏天比春天热。   2) 中国比法国大。
     3) 北京冬天比伦敦冬天冷。   4) 伦敦春天比伦敦冬天漂亮。
     5) 中国菜比 / 没英国菜好吃。   6) 我比我哥哥小。

认读练习 - Matching up

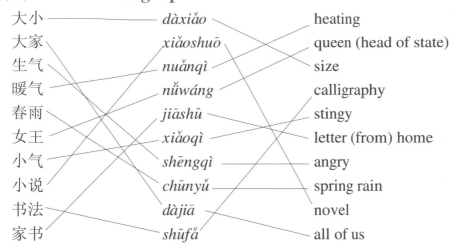

大小	*dàxiǎo*	heating
大家	*xiǎoshuō*	queen (head of state)
生气	*nuǎnqì*	size
暖气	*nǚwáng*	calligraphy
春雨	*jiāshū*	stingy
女王	*xiǎoqì*	letter (from) home
小气	*shēngqì*	angry
小说	*chūnyǔ*	spring rain
书法	*dàjiā*	novel
家书	*shūfǎ*	all of us

翻译练习 - Translation

1. 中国比英国大。
2. 我很喜欢春天，春天不冷不热。
3. 我和我男朋友一样高。
4. 我们（家）的狗没你们（家）的狗大。
5. 烤鸭比牛肉炒青菜贵。
6. 伦敦冬天天气怎么样？伦敦冬天比北京暖和多了。

Lesson Ten

听力练习 - Listening Practice

2. Listen to the short dialogues and choose the right answer for each question.

1) c. 商学院   2) c. 开车   3) c. 看朋友
4) a. 图书馆   5) b. 没有自行车   6) b. 坐火车贵

语法练习 - Grammar Practice

1. Choose the correct word in A, B or C to complete each of the following sentences.

1) b. 坐   2) a. 还书   3) c. 回   4) a. 走   5) c. 怎么   6) b. 来

2. Using appropriate question words to ask questions to the underlined parts.

1) **谁**明天开车去商学院看朋友？
2) 他**哪天**开车去商学院看朋友？

3) 他明天**怎么**去商学院看朋友？

4) 他明天开车去**哪儿**看朋友？

5) 他明天开车去商学院**做什么**？

6) 他明天开车去商学院看**谁**？

认读练习 - Matching up

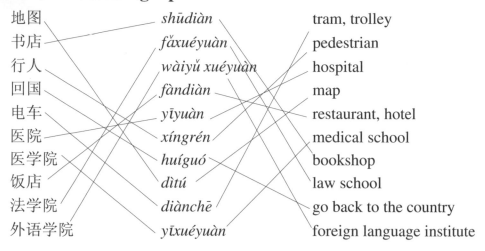

地图	*shūdiàn*	tram, trolley
书店	*fǎxuéyuàn*	pedestrian
行人	*wàiyǔ xuéyuàn*	hospital
回国	*fàndiàn*	map
电车	*yīyuàn*	restaurant, hotel
医院	*xíngrén*	medical school
医学院	*huíguó*	bookshop
饭店	*dìtú*	law school
法学院	*diànchē*	go back to the country
外语学院	*yīxuéyuàn*	foreign language institute

翻译练习 - Translation

1. 我明天不开车去学院。

2. 你去哪儿？我去书店买书。

3. 李先生今天坐地铁回家。

4. 他天天去图书馆看书。

5. 我妈妈不会骑自行车，她天天坐（公共汽）车去上班。

6. 王明明天不来上班，他今天晚上去北京。

Listening Scripts

Lesson One
听力练习 - Listening Practice
1. Listen and choose the phrase you have heard in each group.

　1) 你好　　　　　　　　2) 谢谢
　3) 您好　　　　　　　　4) 再见
　5) 不谢　　　　　　　　6) 我很好

Lesson Two
听力练习 - Listening Practice
Listen to the short dialogues and mark if each of the following sentences is true (T) or false (F).

　1. 女：您贵姓？　　　　　男：我姓李。
　2. 男：你叫什么名字？　　女：我叫王英。
　3. 男：他叫什么名字？　　女：他叫方国伦。
　4. 女：他姓什么？　　　　男：他姓布什。
　5. 女：我叫王英。你叫什么？　男：我叫李贵。
　6. 女：我姓张，你呢？　　男：我也姓张。

Lesson Three
听力练习 - Listening Practice
Listen to the short dialogues and mark if each of the following sentences is true (T) or false (F).

　1. 男：小姐，你叫什么名字？　女：我叫方小英。
　2. 男：谢老师是哪国人？　　女：她是法国人。
　3. 男：王先生是什么地方人？　女：他是北京人。
　4. 男：王太太是医生吗？　　女：不是，她是老师。
　5. 男：方小姐是不是英国人？　女：她是英国人。
　6. 男：他们都是中国人吗？　女：不，他们都不是中国人。

Lesson Four

听力练习 - Listening Practice

Listen to the short dialogues and choose the correct answer for each question.

1. 女：今天几号？　　　　　男：今天十月一号。

   男：What is the date today?

2. 女：王英的生日是哪天？　　男：二月十七日。

   男：When is Wang Ying's birthday?

3. 女：明天是星期二吗？　　　男：不是，明天是星期三。

   男：What day is tomorrow?

4. 女：她是谁？　　　　　　　男：她是王老师，王老师是北京人。

   男：Where is Teacher Wang from?

5. 女：李英，星期六是几号？　男：星期六是六月二十九号。

   男：What is the date this Saturday?

6. 女：今天是谁的生日？　　　男：今天是我弟弟的生日。

   男：Whose birthday is it today?

Lesson Five

听力练习 - Listening Practice

Listen to the short dialogues and mark if each of the following sentences is true (T) or false (F).

1. 男：你学中文吗？　　　　　　女：不，我不学中文。
2. 男：你今天晚上看不看电视？　女：我不看电视，我看书。
3. 男：李英学什么专业？　　　　女：她学英国文学。
4. 男：王京天天晚上都学中文吗？　女：不，他星期天晚上不学。
5. 男：你早上喝什么？　　　　　女：我喝牛奶。
6. 男：你晚上写不写汉字？　　　女：不写，我早上写。

Lesson Six

听力练习 - Listening Practice

2. Listen to the short statements or dialogues and mark if each of the following sentences is true (T) or false (F).

   1) 小李是中国人，他应该会写汉字。
   2) 她喜欢打篮球，可是她不喜欢打网球。

3) 王老师会说汉语、英语，也会说一点儿日语。

4) 女：你认识汉字吗？　　　　　　　　男：我认识汉字，可是我不会写汉字。

5) 女：你喜欢喝什么？　　　　　　　　男：中国茶，我天天早上都喝中国茶。

6) 女：我们晚上一起看电视，好吗？　　男：我今天晚上想看书，不想看电视。

Lesson Seven

听力练习 - Listening Practice

2. Listen to the short dialogues and choose the right answer for each question.

1) 女：先生，您想吃点儿什么？　　　　男：我要一盘炒饭。

　　男：**What did the man want?**

2) 男：小姐，有中国啤酒吗？　　　　　女：对不起，没有，我们只有英国啤酒。

　　男：**What did the restaurant have?**

3) 女：先生，你们这儿什么菜很有名？　男：我们这儿的红烧肉很有名。

　　男：**What is their famous dish?**

4) 女：小王，你喜不喜欢喝中国茶？　　男：我天天都喝中国茶。

　　男：**What does Xiao Wang like to drink?**

5) 男：方小姐，你有中文书吗？　　　　女：没有，我有英文书。

　　男：**What books does Miss Fang have?**

6) 女：星期六是我的生日。　　　　　　男：我们去吃北京烤鸭，好吗？

　　男：**Why are they going out for a meal?**

Lesson Eight

听力练习 - Listening Practice

2. Listen to the short dialogue and choose the right answer for each question.

1) 男：你家有几口人？　　　　女：六口人。

　　男：**How many people are there in her family?**

2) 男：王小明是作家吗？　　　女：对，他是作家。

　　男：**What is Wang Xiaoming's profession?**

3) 男：小李，你饿不饿？　　　女：我不饿，我有点儿渴。

　　男：**Is Xiao Li hungry or thirsty?**

4) 男：王英有哥哥吗？　　　　女：王英有两个弟弟，一个妹妹，可是她没有哥哥。

　　男：**What doesn't Wang Ying have?**

5) 男：你家有猫吗？　　　　　女：我有一条狗，可是我没有猫。

　　男：**How many cats does she have?**

6) 男：你姐姐做什么工作？　　　女：我姐姐是中学老师。

　　男：**What does her elder sister do?**

Lesson Nine

听力练习 - Listening Practice

2. Listen to the short dialogues and choose the right answer for each question.

1) 男：你比你弟弟高吗？　　　　　女：我没有我弟弟高。

　　男：**Who is taller?**

2) 男：伦敦冬天和北京一样冷吗？　女：不，伦敦比北京暖和。

　　男：**Which city is colder - Beijing or London?**

3) 男：你和你姐姐谁高？　　　　　女：我姐姐比我高。

　　男：**Who is taller?**

4) 男：伦敦冬天常常下雨吗？　　　女：不常下。伦敦夏天常常下雨。

　　男：**What season does London often rain?**

5) 男：你喜欢下雪天还是下雨天？　女：我喜欢下雪天。

　　男：**Which kind of weather does the girl like?**

6) 男：英国人多还是法国人多？　　女：法国人多。

　　男：**Which of these places has a bigger population?**

Lesson Ten

听力练习 - Listening Practice

2. Listen to the short dialogues and choose the right answer for each question.

1) 男：你去哪儿？　　　　　　　　女：我去商学院。

　　男：**Where is she going?**

2) 男：你怎么去商学院？　　　　　女：我开车去。

　　男：**How is she going to the Business School?**

3) 男：你来伦敦做什么？　　　　　女：我来看朋友。

　　男：**Why is she in London?**

4) 男：你回家吗？　　　　　　　　女：我先去图书馆再回家。

　　男：**Where is she going first?**

5) 男：你怎么不骑车去商店？　　　女：我没有自行车。

　　男：**Why isn't she going shopping by bike?**

6) 男：小李，你明天怎么不坐火车来　女：坐火车比坐公共汽车贵多了。

　　男：**Why is Xiao Li coming by bus?**

Chinese-English Vocabulary List

吧	ba	pt	an interrogative or suggestive particle	4
八	bā	num	eight	1
爸	bà	n	dad	8
爸爸	bàba	n	dad	8
白	bái	adj	white	7
白菜	báicài	n	Chinese cabbage	7
白酒	báijiǔ	n	liquor	7
班	bān	n	shift	10
杯	bēi	m.w/n	glass of, cup of; cup	7
北	běi	n	north	3
北京	Běijīng	pn	Beijing	3
比	bǐ	v/prep	compare; compared with	9
不	bù	adv	no, not	1
菜	cài	n	vegetable; dish; food	7
茶	chá	n	tea	5
常	cháng	adv	often	9
常常	chángcháng	adv	often	9
炒	chǎo	v	stir fry	7
炒饭	chǎofàn	n	stir-fried rice	7
车	chē	n	vehicle	10
吃	chī	v	eat	7
春	chūn	n	spring	9
春天	chūntiān	n	spring	9
大	dà	adj	big, old	4
打	dǎ	v	play (games); beat	6
打的	dǎdī	v-o	take a taxi	10
的	de	pt	an attributive and possessive particle	4
地	dì	n	place; earth	3
地方	dìfāng	n	place	3
地铁	dìtiě	n	underground train	10
弟	dì	n	younger brother	4
弟弟	dìdi	n	younger brother	4
点	diǎn	n/v	point; hour; order	6, 7

店	diàn	n	shop	10
电	diàn	n/adj	electricity, electric	5
电视	diànshì	n	TV	5
东	dōng	n	east	10
东方	dōngfāng	n	oriental	10
冬	dōng	n	winter	9
冬天	dōngtiān	n	winter	9
都	dōu	adv	all, both	3
对	duì	adj	correct; right	2
对不起	duìbuqǐ	ie	sorry, pardon me	4
多	duō	q.w/adj	how many/much; many, much	4
多了	duōle	comp	much (complement)	9
饿	è	adj	hungry	8
儿	er		non-syllabic diminutive particle	6
二	èr	num	two	1
法	fǎ	n	France, law, method	6
法国	fǎguó	p.n	France	7
法语	fǎyǔ	n	French language	6
饭	fàn	n	cooked rice; food, meal	7
方	fāng	n	Fang (a surname); place	2
方国伦	Fāng Guólún	p.n	Fang Guolun (a name)	2
该	gāi	m.v	should	6
高	gāo	adj	tall (person or building), high	9
哥	gē	n	elder brother	8
哥哥	gēge	n	elder brother	8
个	gè	m.w	for people; general classifier	7
公	gōng	adj	public	10
公共	gōnggòng	adj	public	10
公共汽车	gōnggòng qìchē	n	bus	10
工	gōng	n/v	work, labour	8
工作	gōngzuò	n/v	work	8
共	gòng	adv	together	10
狗	gǒu	n	dog	8
馆	guǎn	n	building	10
贵	guì	adj	honourable; expensive	2

国	guó	n	country	2
还	hái	adv	still	5
还是	háishì	conj	or	5
汉	hàn	n	Chinese	5
汉语	hànyǔ	n	Chinese language	6
汉字	hànzì	n	Chinese character	5
好	hǎo	adj	good; well	1
好吃	hǎochī	adj	delicious	7
号	hào	n	day; number; size	4
喝	hē	v	drink	5
和	hé	conj	and	8
很	hěn	adv	very, rather	1
红	hóng	adj	red	7
红酒	hóngjiǔ	n	red wine	7
红烧肉	hóngshāoròu	n	braised meat in soy sauce	7
欢*	huān		happy	6
还	huán	v	return	10
还书	huán shū	v-o	return books	10
回	huí	v	go back, return	10
回家	huíjiā	v-o	go back home	10
会	huì	m.v/n	can, may; meeting	6
火	huǒ	n	fire	10
火车	huǒchē	n	locomotive, train	10
几	jǐ	q.w	how many (less than 10); several	4
家	jiā	n	home; family; house; specialist in a field	8
见	jiàn	v	see; meet	1
叫	jiào	v	be called; call, shout	2
姐	jiě	n	elder sister	3
今	jīn	n	today, this	4
今年	jīnnián	n	this year	4
今天	jīntiān	n	today	4
京*	jīng	n	capital	2
就	jiù	adv	exactly (emphasis)	3
九	jiǔ	num	nine	1
九月	jiǔyuè	t.w	September	4

酒	jiǔ	n	alcoholic drink	7
开	kāi	v	drive; open, have a meeting	10
开车	kāichē	v-o	drive	10
看	kàn	v	see, watch, read, look	5
烤	kǎo	v	roast; bake	7
烤鸭	kǎoyā	n	roast duck	7
可	kě	m.v	may, can	6
可是	kěshì	conj	but	6
渴	kě	adj	thirsty	8
口	kǒu	m.w/n	for family members; mouth	8
快	kuài	adj/adv	pleased; fast	4
快乐	kuàilè	adj	happy	4
来	lái	v	come	10
篮	lán	n	basket	6
篮球	lánqiú	n	basketball	6
老	lǎo	adj	old	3
老师	lǎoshī	n	teacher	3
了	le	pt	part of a complement	9
乐	lè	adj	happy	4
累	lèi	adj	tired	8
冷	lěng	adj	cold	9
李	lǐ	n	Li (a surname); plum	2
李贵	Lǐ Guì	p.n	Li Gui (a name)	2
李小英	Lǐ Xiǎoyīng	p.n	Li Xiaoying (a name)	2
两	liǎng	num	two (use in front of a measure word)	8
亮	liàng	adj	bright, shiny	9
六	liù	num	six	1
路	lù	n	road, way	10
律	lǜ	n	law; rule	8
律师	lǜshī	n	laywer	8
伦*	lún	n	ethics	2
伦敦	Lúndūn	p.n	London	3
吗	ma	pt	an interrogative particle	1
妈	mā	n	mum	8
妈妈	māma	n	mum	8

忙	máng	adj	busy	8
猫	māo	n	cat	8
么*	me		what	2
没	méi	adv	negation word for 有	7
妹	mèi	n	younger sister	4
妹妹	mèimei	n	younger sister	4
们*	men		plural form of human beings	3
名	míng	n	name	2
名字	míngzi	n	name	2
明	míng	n/adj	next; bright	4
明天	míngtiān	t.w	tomorrow	4
哪	nǎ/něi	q.w	which	3
哪儿	nǎr	q.w	where	10
那	nà/nèi	pron	that	3
奶	nǎi	n	milk	5
男	nán	n	man, male	8
男朋友	nán péngyou	n	boyfriend	8
呢	ne	pt	interrogative particle for follow up questions	2
你	nǐ	pron	you	1
你们	nǐmen	pron	you	3
年	nián	n	year	4
您	nín	pron	you (polite form)	1
牛	niú	n	cow, ox	5
牛奶	niúnǎi	n	milk	5
牛肉	niúròu	n	beef	7
女	nǚ	n	woman	8
女朋友	nǚ péngyou	n	girlfriend	8
暖	nuǎn	adj	warm	9
暖和	nuǎnhuo	adj	warm	9
盘	pán	m.w/n	dish of, plate of; plate	7
胖	pàng	adj	stout; fat	9
朋	péng	n	friend	8
朋友	péngyou	n	friend	8
啤*	pí		beer	7
啤酒	píjiǔ	n	beer	7

漂*	piào	adj	smart	9
漂亮	piàoliang	adj	pretty	9
瓶	píng	m.w/n	bottle of; bottle	7
七	qī	num	seven	1
期	qī	n	period	4
骑	qí	v	horse-ride	10
气	qì	n	air; breath	9
起*	qǐ	v	rise	4
汽	qì	n	steam	10
汽车	qìchē	n	automobile	10
青	qīng	adj	green	7
青菜	qīngcài	n	green vegetable	7
球	qiú	n	ball	6
秋	qiū	n	autumn	9
秋天	qiūtiān	n	autumn	9
去	qù	v	go (opposite direction of 来)	10
热	rè	adj	hot	9
人	rén	n	person, people	3
认	rèn	v	recognise	6
认识	rènshi	v	know	6
日	rì	n	day (formal); sun; Japanese	4
日语	rìyǔ	n	Japanese language	6
肉	ròu	n	meat	7
三	sān	num	three	1
商	shāng	n/adj	business; commercial	8
商店	shāngdiàn	n	shop	10
商人	shāngrén	n	businessman	8
商学院	shāngxuéyuàn	n	business school	10
上	shàng	prep/v	on; go on	5
上班	shànbān	v/n	go to work	10
上网	shàngwǎng	v	surf the net	5
烧	shāo	v	cook; braise	7
少	shǎo	adj	few; little	9
什*	shén		what	2
什么	shénme	q.w	what	2

生	shēng	v	give birth to	3
生日	shēngrì	n	birthday	4
师	shī	n	master	3
十	shí	num	ten	1
十一月	shíyīyuè	t.w	November	4
识	shí	v	know	6
是	shì	v	be	3
视	shì	n/v	vision; watch	5
瘦	shòu	adj	thin (a person)	9
书	shū	n	book	5
谁	shuí/shéi	q.w	who	3
说	shuō	v/n	speak	6
四	sì	num	four	1
岁	suì	m.w/n	year (age); time	4
他	tā	pron	he; him	2
他们	tāmen	pron	they, them	3
她	tā	pron	she; her	2
太	tài	n/adv	wife; too (excessive)	3
太太	tàitai	n	Mrs, wife	3
踢	tī	v	kick; play (football)	6
天	tiān	n	day, sky	4
天气	tiānqì	n	weather	9
天天	tiāntiān	adv	every day	5
条	tiáo	m.w/n	for various long narrow things	8
铁	tiě	n	iron	10
图	tú	n	map; picture	10
图书馆	túshūguǎn	n	library	10
外	wài	n	foreign; outside	6
外语	wàiyǔ	n	foreign language	6
晚	wǎn	adj/adv	late	5
晚上	wǎnshang	n	evening	5
碗	wǎn	m.w/n	bowl of; bowl	7
王	wáng	n	Wang (a surname); king	2
王京	Wáng Jīng	p.n	Wang Jing (Jim King)(a name)	2
网	wǎng	n	net	5

网球	wǎngqiú	n	tennis	6
为	wèi	prep	for, on account of	6
为什么	wèishénme	q.w	why	6
文	wén	n	(written) language	5
文学	wénxué	n	literature	5
我	wǒ	pron	I; me	1
我们	wǒmen	pron	we, us	3
五	wǔ	num	five	1
五星啤酒	wǔxīngpíjiǔ	n	Five Stars Beer	7
喜*	xǐ		like	6
喜欢	xǐhuan	m.v/v	like	6
下	xià	v	fall, get off	9
下雪	xiàxuě	v-o	snow	9
下雨	xiàyǔ	v-o	rain	9
夏	xià	n	summer	9
夏天	xiàtiān	n	summer	9
想	xiǎng	m.v	would like to, intend; think; miss	6
先生	xiānsheng	n	Mr; husband	3
小	xiǎo	adj	small; young	2
小姐	xiǎojie	n	Miss	3
写	xiě	v	write	5
谢	xiè	v/n	thank; Xie (a surname)	1
星	xīng	n	star	4
星期	xīngqī	n/m.w	week	4
星期二	xīngqī'èr	t.w	Tuesday	4
行	xíng	v	walk; shop	10
姓	xìng	v	be surnamed	2
学	xué	v/n	learn, study	5
学生	xuésheng	n	student	8
学院	xuéyuàn	n	college	10
雪	xuě	v	snow	9
鸭	yā	n	duck	7
样*	yàng	m.w/n	type; manner	9
要	yào	v	want	7
也	yě	adv	also; too; neither	2

业	yè	n	course, industry	5
一	yī	num	one	1
一起	yīqǐ	adv	together	6
一样	yīyàng	adj/adv	the same	9
一点儿	yīdiǎnr	n	a bit	6
医	yī	n/v	medicine; to cure	3
医生	yīshēng	n	doctor	3
因	yīn	n	cause, reason for	6
因为	yīnwèi	conj	because	6
应	yīng	m.v	should; respond	6
应该	yīnggāi	m.v	should	6
英*	yīng	n	hero; Britain	2
英国	Yīngguó	p.n	UK	3
英文	yīngwén	n	English language	5
有	yǒu	v	have, there be	7
有点儿	yǒudiǎnr	adv	somewhat; a bit	8
有名	yǒumíng	adj	famous	7
友	yǒu	n	friend	8
语	yǔ	n	language	6
雨	yǔ	n	rain	9
院	yuàn	n	compound; courtyard	10
月	yuè	n	month, moon	4
再	zài	adv	again; later	1
再见	zàijiàn	id	bye, see you again	1
早	zǎo	adj/adv	early	5
早上	zǎoshang	n	morning	5
怎*	zěn		how; why	9
怎么	zěnme	adv	how	10
怎么样	zěnmeyàng	q.w	how is it?	9
这	zhè/zhèi	pron	this	3
这儿	zhèr	l.w	here	8
只	zhī	m.w	for birds and some other animals	7
只	zhǐ	adv	only	7
中	zhōng	n	middle	3
中国	Zhōngguó	p.n	China	3

中文	zhōngwén	n	Chinese language	5
专	zhuān	adj	specialised	5
专业	zhuānyè	n	major, subject	5
字	zì	n	character	2
自*	zì		self	10
自行车	zìxíngchē	n	bike	10
走	zǒu	v	walk	10
走路	zǒulù	v-o	walk	10
足	zú	n	foot	6
足球	zúqiú	n	football	6
做	zuò	v	make, do	5
坐	zuò	v	sit, take	10
作	zuò	v	do; make; write	8
作家	zuòjiā	n	writer	8

English-Chinese Vocabulary List

a bit	一点儿	yīdiǎnr	n	6
again; later	再	zài	adv	1
air; breath	气	qì	n	9
alcoholic drink	酒	jiǔ	n	7
all, both	都	dōu	adv	3
also; too; neither	也	yě	adv	2
an attributive and possessive particle	的	de	pt	4
an interrogative or suggestive particle	吧	ba	pt	4
an interrogative particle	吗	ma	pt	1
and	和	hé	conj	8
automobile	汽车	qìchē	n	10
autumn	秋	qiū	n	9
autumn	秋天	qiūtiān	n	9
ball	球	qiú	n	6
basket	篮	lán	n	6
basketball	篮球	lánqiú	n	6
be	是	shì	v	3
be called; call, shout	叫	jiào	v	2
be surnamed	姓	xìng	v	2
because	因为	yīnwèi	conj	6
beef	牛肉	niúròu	n	7
beer	啤*	pí		7
beer	啤酒	píjiǔ	n	7
Beijing	北京	Běijīng	pn	3
big, old	大	dà	adj	4
bike	自行车	zìxíngchē	n	10
birthday	生日	shēngrì	n	4
book	书	shū	n	5
bottle of; bottle	瓶	píng	m.w/n	7
bowl of; bowl	碗	wǎn	m.w/n	7
boyfriend	男朋友	nán péngyou	n	8
braised meat in soy sauce	红烧肉	hóngshāoròu	n	7
bright, shiny	亮	liàng	adj	9
building	馆	guǎn	n	10

CHINESE IN STEPS appendices

137

bus	公共汽车	gōnggòng qìchē	n	10
business school	商学院	shāngxuéyuàn	n	10
business; commercial	商	shāng	n/adj	8
businessman	商人	shāngrén	n	8
busy	忙	máng	adj	8
but	可是	kěshì	conj	6
bye, see you again	再见	zàijiàn	id	1
can, may; meeting	会	huì	m.v/n	6
capital	京*	jīng	n	2
cat	猫	māo	n	8
cause, reason for	因	yīn	n	6
character	字	zì	n	2
China	中国	Zhōngguó	p.n	3
Chinese	汉	hàn	n	5
Chinese cabbage	白菜	báicài	n	7
Chinese character	汉字	hànzì	n	5
Chinese language	中文	zhōngwén	n	5
Chinese language	汉语	hànyǔ	n	6
cold	冷	lěng	adj	9
college	学院	xuéyuàn	n	10
come	来	lái	v	10
compare; compared with	比	bǐ	v/prep	9
compound; courtyard	院	yuàn	n	10
cook; braise	烧	shāo	v	7
cooked rice; food, meal	饭	fàn	n	7
correct; right	对	duì	v	2
country	国	guó	n	2
course, industry	业	yè	n	5
cow, ox	牛	niú	n	5
dad	爸	bà	n	8
dad	爸爸	bàba	n	8
day (formal); sun; Japanese	日	rì	n	4
day, sky	天	tiān	n	4
day; number; size	号	hào	n	4
delicious	好吃	hǎochī	adj	7
dish of, plate of; plate	盘	pán	m.w/n	7
do; make; write	作	zuò	v	8

doctor	医生	yīshēng	n	3
dog	狗	gǒu	n	8
drink	喝	hē	v	5
drive	开车	kāichē	v-o	10
drive; open, have a meeting	开	kāi	v	10
duck	鸭	yā	n	7
early	早	zǎo	adj/adv	5
east	东	dōng	n	10
eat	吃	chī	v	7
eight	八	bā	num	1
elder brother	哥	gē	n	8
elder brother	哥哥	gēge	n	8
elder sister	姐	jěi	n	3
electricity, electric	电	diàn	n/adj	5
English language	英文	yīngwén	n	5
ethics	伦*	lún	n	2
evening	晚上	wǎnshang	n	5
every day	天天	tiāntiān	adv	5
exactly (emphasis)	就	jiù	adv	3
fall, get off	下	xià	v	9
famous	有名	yǒumíng	adj	7
Fang (a surname); place	方	fāng	n	2
Fang Guolun (a name)	方国伦	Fāng Guólún	p.n	2
few; little	少	shǎo	adj	9
fire	火	huǒ	n	10
first	先	xiān	adv	3
five	五	wǔ	num	1
Five Stars Beer	五星啤酒	wǔxīngpíjiǔ	n	7
foot	足	zú	n	6
football	足球	zúqiú	n	6
for birds and some other animals	只	zhī	m.w	7
for family members; mouth	口	kǒu	m.w/n	8
for people; general classifier	个	gè	m.w	7
for various long narrow things	条	tiáo	m.w/n	8
for, on account of	为	wèi	prep	6
foreign language	外语	wàiyǔ	n	6
foreign; outside	外	wài	n	6

four	四	sì	num	1
France	法国	fǎguó	p.n	7
France, law, method	法	fǎ	n	6
French language	法语	fǎyǔ	n	6
friend	友	yǒu	n	8
friend	朋	péng	n	8
friend	朋友	péngyou	n	8
girlfriend	女朋友	nǚ péngyou	n	8
give birth to	生	shēng	v	3
glass of, cup of; cup	杯	bēi	m.w/n	7
go (opposite direction of 来)	去	qù	v	10
go back home	回家	huíjiā	v-o	10
go back, return	回	huí	v	10
go to work	上班	shàngbān	v/n	10
good; well	好	hǎo	adj	1
green	青	qīng	adj	7
green vegetable	青菜	qīngcài	n	7
happy	乐	lè	adj	4
happy	快乐	kuàilè	adj	4
happy	欢*	huān		6
have, there be	有	yǒu	v	7
he; him	他	tā	pron	2
here	这儿	zhèr	l.w	8
hero; Britain	英*	yīng	n	2
home; family; house; specialist in a field	家	jiā	n	8
honourable; expensive	贵	guì	adj	2
horse-ride	骑	qí	v	10
hot	热	rè	adj	9
how	怎么	zěnme	adv	10
how is it?	怎么样	zěnmeyàng	q.w	9
how many (less than 10); several	几	jǐ	q.w	4
how many/much; many, much	多	duō	q.w/adj	4
how; why	怎*	zěn		9
hungry	饿	è	adj	8
I; me	我	wǒ	pron	1
interrogative particle for follow up questions	呢	ne	pt	2
iron	铁	tiě	n	10

Japanese language	日语	rìyǔ	n	6
kick; play (football)	踢	tī	v	6
know	认识	rènshi	v	6
know	识	shí	v	6
language	语	yǔ	n	6
late	晚	wǎn	adj/adv	5
law; rule	律	lù	n	8
laywer	律师	lùshī	n	8
learn, study	学	xué	v/n	5
Li (a surname); plum	李	lǐ	n	2
Li Gui (a name)	李贵	Lǐ Guì	p.n	2
Li Xiaoying (a name)	李小英	Lǐ Xiǎoyīng	p.n	2
library	图书馆	túshūguǎn	n	10
like	喜*	xǐ		6
like	喜欢	xǐhuan	m.v/v	6
liquor	白酒	báijiǔ	n	7
literature	文学	wénxué	n	5
locomotive, train	火车	huǒchē	n	10
London	伦敦	Lúndūn	p.n	3
major, subject	专业	zhuānyè	n	5
make, do	做	zuò	v	5
man, male	男	nán	n	8
map; picture	图	tú	n	10
master	师	shī	n	3
may, can	可	kě	m.v	6
meat	肉	ròu	n	7
medicine; to cure	医	yī	n/v	3
middle	中	zhōng	n	3
milk	奶	nǎi	n	5
milk	牛奶	niúnǎi	n	5
Miss	小姐	xiǎojie	n	3
month, moon	月	yuè	n	4
morning	早上	zǎoshang	n	5
Mr; husband	先生	xiānsheng	n	3
Mrs, wife	太太	tàitai	n	3
much (complement)	多了	duōle		9
mum	妈	mā	n	8

mum	妈妈	māma	n	8
name	名	míng	n	2
name	名字	míngzi	n	2
negation word for 有	没	méi	adv	7
net	网	wǎng	n	5
next; bright	明	míng	n/adj	4
nine	九	jiǔ	num	1
no, not	不	bù	adv	1
non-syllabic diminutive particle	儿	er		6
north	北	běi	n	3
November	十一月	shíyīyuè	t.w	4
often	常	cháng	adv	9
often	常常	chángcháng	adv	9
old	老	lǎo	adj	3
on; go on	上	shàng	prep/v	5
one	一	yī	num	1
only	只	zhǐ	adv	7
or	还是	háishì	conj	5
oriental	东方	dōngfāng	n	10
part of a complement	了	le	pt	9
period	期	qī	n	4
person, people	人	rén	n	3
place	地方	dìfāng	n	3
place; earth	地	dì	n	3
play (games); beat	打	dǎ	v	6
pleased; fast	快	kuài	adj/adv	4
plural form of human beings	们*	men		3
point; hour; order	点	diǎn	n/v	6, 7
pretty	漂亮	piàoliang	adj	9
public	公	gōng	adj	10
public	公共	gōnggòng	adj	10
rain	下雨	xiàyǔ	v-o	9
rain	雨	yǔ	n	9
recognise	认	rèn	v	6
red	红	hóng	adj	7
red wine	红酒	hóngjiǔ	n	7
return	还	huán	v	10

return books	还书	huán shū	v-o	10
rise	起*	qǐ	v	4
road, way	路	lù	n	10
roast duck	烤鸭	kǎoyā	n	7
roast; bake	烤	kǎo	v	7
see, watch, read, look	看	kàn	v	5
see; meet	见	jiàn	v	1
self	自*	zì		10
September	九月	jiǔyuè	t.w	4
seven	七	qī	num	1
she; her	她	tā	pron	2
shift	班	bān	n	10
shop	商店	shāngdiàn	n	10
shop	店	diàn	n	10
should	应该	yīnggāi	m.v	6
should	该	gāi	m.v	6
should; respond	应	yīng	m.v	6
sit, take	坐	zuò	v	10
six	六	liù	num	1
small; young	小	xiǎo	adj	2
smart	漂*	piào	adj	9
snow	下雪	xiàxuě	v-o	9
snow	雪	xuě	v	9
somewhat; a bit	有点儿	yǒudiǎnr	adv	8
sorry, pardon me	对不起	duìbuqǐ	id	4
speak	说	shuō	v/n	6
specialised	专	zhuān	adj	5
spring	春	chūn	n	9
spring	春天	chūntiān	n	9
star	星	xīng	n	4
steam	汽	qì	n	10
still	还	hái	adv	5
stir fry	炒	chǎo	v	7
stir-fried rice	炒饭	chǎofàn	n	7
stout; fat	胖	pàng	adj	9
student	学生	xuésheng	n	8
summer	夏	xià	n	9

summer	夏天	xiàtiān	n	9
surf the net	上网	shàngwǎng	v	5
take a taxi	打的	dǎdī	v-o	10
tall (person or building), high	高	gāo	adj	9
tea	茶	chá	n	5
teacher	老师	lǎoshī	n	3
ten	十	shí	num	1
tennis	网球	wǎngqiú	n	6
thank; Xie (a surname)	谢	xiè	v/n	1
that	那	nà/nèi	pron	3
the same	一样	yīyàng	adj/adv	9
they, them	他们	tāmen	pron	3
thin (a person)	瘦	shòu	adj	9
thirsty	渴	kě	adj	8
this	这	zhè/zhèi	pron	3
this year	今年	jīnnián	n	4
three	三	sān	num	1
tired	累	lèi	adj	8
today	今天	jīntiān	n	4
today, this	今	jīn	n	4
together	一起	yīqǐ	adv	6
together	共	gòng	adv	10
tomorrow	明天	míngtiān	t.w	4
Tuesday	星期二	xīngqī'èr	t.w	4
TV	电视	diànshì	n	5
two	二	èr	num	1
two (use in front of a measure word)	两	liǎng	num	8
type; manner	样*	yàng	m.w/n	9
UK	英国	Yīngguó	p.n	3
underground train	地铁	dìtiě	n	10
vegetable; dish; food	菜	cài	n	7
vehicle	车	chē	n	10
very, rather	很	hěn	adv	1
vision; watch	视	shì	n/v	5
walk	走	zǒu	v	10
walk	走路	zǒulù	v-o	10
walk; shop	行	xíng	v	10

Wang (a surname); king	王	wáng	n	2
Wang Jing (Jim King) (a name)	王京	Wáng Jīng	p.n	2
want	要	yào	v	7
warm	暖	nuǎn	adj	9
warm	暖和	nuǎnhuo	adj	9
we, us	我们	wǒmen	pron	3
weather	天气	tiānqì	n	9
week	星期	xīngqī	n/m.w	4
what	么*	me		2
what	什么	shénme	q.w	2
what	什*	shén		2
where	哪儿	nǎr	q.w	10
which	哪	nǎ/něi	q.w	3
white	白	bái	adj	7
who	谁	shuí/shéi	q.w	3
why	为什么	wèishénme	q.w	6
wife; too (excessive)	太	tài	n/adv	3
winter	冬	dōng	n	9
winter	冬天	dōngtiān	n	9
woman	女	nǚ	n	8
work	工作	gōngzuò	n/v	8
work, labour	工	gōng	n/v	8
would like to, intend; think; miss	想	xiǎng	m.v	6
write	写	xiě	v	5
writer	作家	zuòjiā	n	8
written language	文	wén	n	5
year	年	nián	n	4
year (age); time	岁	suì	m.w/n	4
you	你	nǐ	pron	1
you	你们	nǐmen	pron	3
you (polite form)	您	nín	pron	1
younger brother	弟	dì	n	4
younger brother	弟弟	dìdi	n	4
younger sister	妹	mèi	n	4
younger sister	妹妹	mèimei	n	4

CHINESE IN STEPS appendices

Word Game

How many Chinese words and phrases can you find in the following table? They are formed only with the neighbouring characters, but characters can be used more than once, and the formation can be in any direction, up down, left right, or vice verse, and diagonally too.

视	踢	的	打	人	铁	地	方	东	北
没	电	足	篮	吧	下	汽	火	红	京
店	书	看	球	网	上	班	车	烧	烤
友	朋	女	王	做	晚	早	吃	肉	鸭
好	男	国	律	炒	饭	白	喝	牛	奶
医	中	学	法	师	生	菜	酒	啤	茶
中	生	文	语	老	人	红	青	杯	碗
先	日	字	汉	小	天	有	字	回	大
岁	月	亮	姐	天	气	名	专	家	会
年	漂	妹	期	今	明	业	作	开	没
饭	五	星	去	年	好	商	店	公	有
馆	多	球	回	很	累	人	雪	共	打
书	少	来	冷	贵	春	雨	下	汽	开
图	猫	狗	热	姓	骑	自	行	车	坐

Dr George X Zhang is the Chinese courses co-ordinator at the Language Centre, School of Oriental and African Studies. He has over twenty years' experience working in British and Chinese universities with interest in language acquisition, cross cultural communications and teacher training. He was awarded a professorship in language education by a Chinese university in 1994.

Linda M Li is a senior lecturer in Chinese and the subject leader in Oriental Culture and Business Development in the European Business School London. She has taught English and Chinese in secondary, tertiary and higher education in China and the UK with interest in applied linguistics, social linguistics and language teaching for business purposes.

Lik Suen is senior lector in Chinese at China and Inner Asia Department, School of Oriental and African Studies. She is a graduate of Beijing Language Institute and has nearly 15 years experience of teaching Chinese as a foreign language at universities in China, Hong Kong and London. She is studying for a PhD in applied linguistics at University of London.